ARCTIC EXODUS

The Last Great Trail Drive

Dick North

For Mike & Elizabeth
with best wishes
Dick North
Dawson City, Y.T.
July 10, '97

Macmillan of Canada
A Division of Canada Publishing Corporation
Toronto, Ontario, Canada

Canadian Cataloguing in Publication Data
North, Dick
Arctic exodus

Includes bibliographical references and index.
ISBN 0-7715-9128-4

1. Reindeer herding – Canada, Northern. I. Title.

SF401.R4N6 1991 636.2'94 C90-095833-2

1 2 3 4 5 JD 95 94 93 92 91

Jacket design: Don Fernley
Jacket photo: Fred Bruemmer
Maps: Full Spectrum Art Inc.

Macmillan of Canada
A Division of Canada Publishing Corporation
Toronto, Ontario, Canada

Printed and bound in Canada
by John Deyell Company

Other books by the same author:

The Mad Trapper of Rat River
The Lost Patrol
Trackdown: The Search for the Mad Trapper

CONTENTS

LIST OF MAPS

FOREWORD

[Will Rogers, part Indian, ex-cowboy, champion trick roper, lecturer, homespun philosopher and humorist, and celebrated movie actor, was also a columnist for the New York *Times* News Service. Shortly before his death in a plane crash in 1935, Will Rogers had written a column about the reindeer drive, excerpts from which are quoted herein. There are a few inaccuracies, and of course, the spelling is pure Rogers, but the gist of the story is there. Will, being an ex-cowhand, fully comprehended how great a feat the reindeer drive really was.]

REINDEER

by Will Rogers

(*Seattle Times*, March 17, 1935)

"Well all I know is just what I read in the papers. Here was an interesting thing that was just lately completed. That fellow who drove that herd of rheindeer clear across Alaska, moving them for domestic animals to tribes away up near the Artic Ocean, he drove em from some place away down in Alaska to just a niblick shot from the North Pole. He was over five years making the trip. I think he had about three thousand when he left, and he raised as many as he lost. And he got there with more than he left with. He was one whole year just getting over one mountain range and river. It will keep those people, Esquimos, away up there from starving. Will give them a start in raising these wonderful animals.

"This fellow that did this was over seventy years old. His drivers used to come and tell him we are lost, and he would say you can see me cant you, well then you are not lost.

"There used to be some wonderful cattle drives from Texas to Montana, Wyoming and even to the Canadian Border. But not a five year one . . .

"These old rheindeer cow boys dident go on a horse either. They go afoot, or on skeis, or skates or something. You know these guys throw a rope too . . . Its a long rawhide one, and they just bundle it all in one hand and throw it out there like throwing rubbish out of a window and then commence to hauling it in, and they say they are awful apt to have a rheindeer on the end of it.

"I never have been to that Alaska. I am crazy to go up there some time . . ."

PROLOGUE

Called by many persons familiar with the livestock industry the most spectacular trail drive in the history of North America, the five-year hegira of three thousand reindeer under the guidance of Laplander Andrew Bahr (known later as "The Arctic Moses") was to win a permanent niche in the lore of the North as one of the great feats of modern times.

Before the drive was over, Bahr and his Eskimo and Lapp reindeer punchers had pushed the herd a distance of over one thousand miles on the map (possibly double that, in actuality), through several mountain ranges, over countless leagues of river-threaded tundra and muskeg, and across the treacherous winter ice of Mackenzie Bay, to deliver the deer to the Canadian government at Kittigazuit, Northwest Territories.

The land was tough enough, but the latitude of the area in which the drive took place insured endless blizzards and bulb-shattering low temperatures in the winter. These extremes were matched in summer by a torrid, never-setting sun that blistered the land on cloudless days and bred a mosquito population that was so dense the winged pests hovered over the herd like a giant, whirling parasol under which both men and animals huddled in mutual misery.

In addition, the characteristics of reindeer — which make a mule, by comparison, look like a paragon of cooperation — guaranteed a pattern of distractions that persisted on a daily basis until the drive was finally concluded in 1935.

Reindeer do not like descent; they are inclined to walk into the wind; they are skittish about predators and imagined predators; they have an inherited instinct to return to the area of their birth; and they are "groupies" and will mingle and depart with any large band of caribou that happens along. The herd in this great exodus, because it was made up mostly of yearlings, displayed many of a reindeer's most recalcitrant characteristics. This all but insured trouble from the start, and extended the journey by three long years.

The incentive for the drive derived from a nagging need for a permanent food source for natives living along Canada's Arctic coast. Mentors in Ottawa, after a prolonged and thorough study involving historical, sociological, and scientific research, concluded that introducing a reindeer industry would help solve the problem.

The elements that eventually made up the components of this industry in North America form a complex pattern consisting of prehistoric glacial cataclysms, geographical differences, and cultural migration and evolution. Thirty thousand years ago, according to the latest archaeological finds, the first humans to enter North America crossed the land bridge that connected Siberia to Alaska. These peoples moved toward the beckoning wilderness as nomadic hunters, content to live on the ungulates that were the predecessors of our present-day caribou, buffalo, moose, and deer. Sixteen millenniums later, waters from huge polar glaciers of the last ice age began to melt, eventually swamping the land bridge to create Bering Strait. This effectively severed the connection between Asia and North America.

The outcome of this division was the inception of slight physical differences between reindeer and caribou, as well as the evolution of contrasting methods of harvesting the animals among Eurasian and North American peoples.

The caribou is slightly larger, more inclined to be of a standard, tawny colour, and sports a longer nose as compared with the flatter, dish-faced appearance of reindeer. More importantly, caribou remained wild and resisted domestication. Reindeer, in contrast, have a long history of being handled, and can be managed like any other farm animal.

Wild reindeer were first domesticated on the taiga of northern Asia and Europe in prehistoric times, affording indigenous peoples meat, fresh milk, skins for clothing and household use, and transportation as draft animals pulling sleds or packing supplies. From time immemorial they have served their masters in a manner similar to yaks in Nepal and Tibet, or water buffalo in southern Asia.

The value of reindeer, and the reason for their long survival as domesticated animals, is that they can thrive on land which is virtually useless to the conventional rancher. Neither cattle, horses, goats, sheep, nor any other domestic grazing animal can survive on the tundra.

Reindeer are, nonetheless, one of the most widely distributed domesticated mammals in the world and, other than their legendary tie-in with Santa Claus, one of the least known. They thrive along the entire polar rim, existing on the northern prairie that extends from Scandinavia across the breadth of Siberia to the Bering Strait. In North America, their cousin the caribou roams across an expanse that stretches eastward for four thousand miles from Alaska to the Atlantic Ocean. The fact that caribou are wild meant that harvesting them was always a hit-or-miss proposition, with natives living well in good years when the caribou came, and living poorly or actually starving in the bad years when the caribou did not show up.

In the early years of this century, the activities of white men in the North began to have a more visible impact on native life. The Canadian government, therefore, resolved to turn the nomadic Inuit peoples, barely out of a Stone-Age lifestyle, into ranchers of the North, and solve problems of employment and subsistence at the same time. The ensuing exodus, the last enduring trail drive in North America, was the result.

When the last roundup has been held on the ranges of the South; when the last grasslands of Texas have been sown to cotton, wheat, or corn; when the cowboys are all [gone], and sheep and cattle are fed from cribs, there will still be grazing animals on the tundras of the North. For this is one part of the world that the plow will never invade. It is the last and continuing land of the roundup.

From "Towards a Self-Sustaining North,"
Canadian Magazine, June 1938

To
Lowell Thomas, Sr., his son, Lowell,
and Amos Burg, my sponsors in
the Explorers Club,
and to the late governor, Bill Egan:
they never lost faith in the Arctic;
and to my children,
Tim, Tam, and Scott

PART ONE

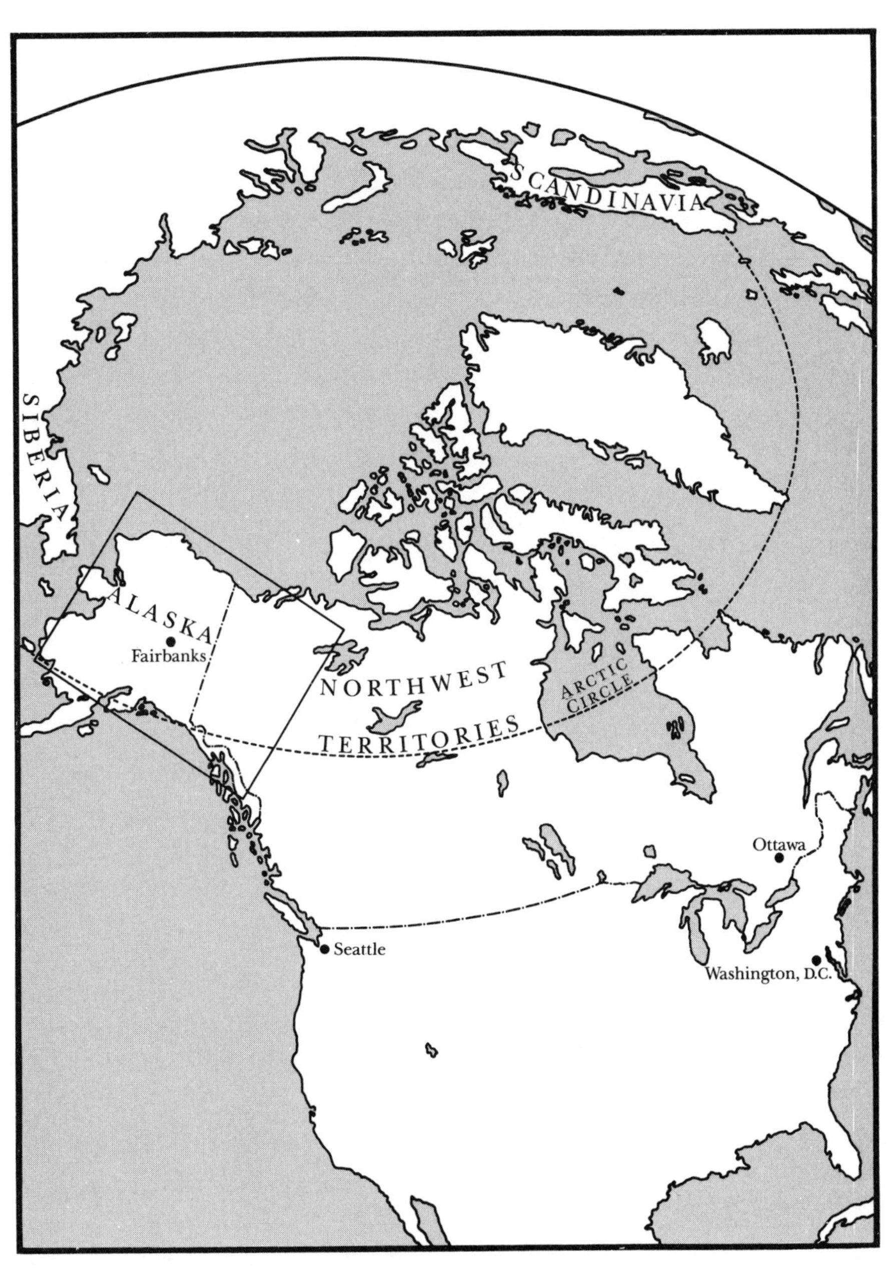

POLAR PERSPECTIVE

CHAPTER 1

The Great Want

Caucasians, with their advanced civilization, should have been well prepared when they first undertook exploration in a region as severe as the Arctic four centuries ago; yet just the opposite was the case. The history of northern exploration is such a litany of disaster it reminds one of so many lemmings in a periodic, suicidal rush to the sea.

The roll call of the dead is a long one, peaking with the loss of one hundred thirty-five men of the Sir John Franklin expedition from sickness, hypothermia, and starvation circa 1848 and 1849.[1] Numerous subsequent expeditions, some searching for Franklin, and others, like him, looking for a route through the Northwest Passage, also lost men.

One of the worst debacles occurred in 1848 when the American-sponsored Lady Franklin Bay expedition to set up a geographical research station on northern Ellesmere Island was cut off from its base of supplies for two years by the raging ice pack. The men were forced to walk out to a predetermined haven on open water where they could expect an emergency relief ship to look for them. The upshot was a trek that accounted for the deaths of seventeen men.

Failure to properly prepare, and survive, by amateurs in the Arctic was one thing, but how about those permanent residents of the region who supposedly thrived in the rugged environment — the Eskimos, or Inuit as they prefer to be called today, and the more northern of Indian tribes of North America? Not surprisingly, theirs, too, is a history of hardship.

The very nature of subsistence by hunting made it, at best, a precarious way of life. For example, a persistent wind from the south at the wrong time of the year could blow the ice pack far out to sea, making it impossible for the Inuit to travel across the floes in search of sea mammals upon which they lived. Starvation frequently resulted.

Similar problems, though with a different twist, plagued hunters who lived inland. Variations in the conditions of weather and vegetation could so affect the route of a migrating caribou herd, that in some years the caribou would veer off in a completely unexpected direction, many miles from their usual path. Then it was up to the hunters to find them. If they were unsuccessful, they starved. Many factors, or a combination of them, could contribute to the change of route: fires that destroyed the lichen upon which the caribou grazed; ice conditions that prevented feeding; huge die-offs from blizzards at fawning time; a sudden proliferation of insects; or the spread of disease, could destroy or divert the herd. Unforeseen hunting pressure by predators, both man and animal, could alter the route of the caribou. Even if the caribou did come, there could be problems of harvesting them if they were not spotted immediately. Biologist Doug Wing, recently following caribou by collar radios, pinpointed a herd at one spot on a given day, and found them sixty miles away the next. Even though feeding, a herd can move along at a deceptively fast gait.

The lifestyle for those nomadic hunters who depended on caribou for survival was a vulnerable one, sometimes, it must have seemed, as unpredictable as the lives of the animals upon which they depended. These people were doubtlessly aware of the limitations of their old ways, and consequently were extremely susceptible when they were exposed to what appeared to be a more efficient life style. Little did they know that their rugged existence was the source of the hardiness and power of their race, or that the haphazard and partial adoption of the white man's culture would leave them in a position worse than either complete adoption, or total rejection, of alien customs.

The northern natives, therefore, suffered considerably when European culture and technology collided with their way of life, commencing with the sixteenth-century intrusion of whaling ships into the eastern Arctic, and later when the same fraternity set up trade along polar coasts of Alaska and the western Arctic. In the 1800s, the barren grounds, the soft underbelly of the Arctic, was pierced by traders from the south. Intrepid adventurers floated down inland rivers such as the mighty Mackenzie which flowed north to the Arctic Ocean, and set up shop. The result of this thrust was a severe economic and sociological impact on the people of the region.

Operators of trading posts were primarily after pelts, meat, and hides, while the sea-borne trade concentrated on whales, and later, seal skins. The sailing merchants traded with the natives to supplement their limited rations aboard ship. This, in turn, gave rise to widespread barter which saw guns, ammunition, and traps exchanged with the native tribes, with predictable results. This commerce tended to destabilize the aboriginal society for a number of reasons. First, the new implements tempted the hunters to over-harvest subsistence animals, thus decimating the very resources they relied on for survival. Second, coastal traders often induced dependency by steering their native customers away from natural diets into foods traditionally unused and unneeded, such as flour, sugar, or later, processed foods. Even worse was the introduction of alcohol, which broke down the family unit because those afflicted with the habit could not hunt, leaving their families to make out as best they could dealing with the trading posts, or whaling ships that wintered in the vicinity.

The ultimate shock for the natives came when substitute materials such as plastics and petroleum replaced the items the whalers were after — whale bone (baleen) and whale oil. Most of the whalers pulled out of the Arctic, leaving the Inuit dependent upon foods they could not replace and goods unessential for survival, yet lacking the survival skills that had atrophied during the trading interlude. Lack of bullets for a rifle with which to shoot a seal, among people who had forgotten how to use a harpoon, would lead to starvation just as surely as if the animal were not there. As a more trivial example, it is worth noting that one of the more popular items purchased by Inuit along the Arctic coast early in the twentieth century was the gramophone, a spring-operated record player.

Farther south, fluctuations in the market prices of furs, and changes in fashions, dictated the life style of the Indian peoples. The relative benevolence and intervention of government agencies and departments, too, seemed to rise and fall as inevitably as the tides.

The havoc wrought by such changeable conditions within a short time attracted the attentive eyes of those men who followed in the wake of the whalers and traders. These were the missionaries, one of whom, Dr. Sheldon Jackson, while investigating cases of famine in Alaska, sought a solution to the vagaries of the nomadic hunters' precarious existence.

Jackson, a bewhiskered, intrepid veteran of a lifetime working with the Indian peoples of the American west, was posted to Alaska in 1877. Eight years later he was appointed the United States General Agent for Education in the new territory. He also continued his missionary work for the Presbyterian church.

In his dual position, Jackson became aware of the plight of the natives and isolated three problems he considered paramount. These were: absence of the Christian religion, the lack of education, and recurring bouts with starvation. Jackson solved the first two, since they were parallel in nature, by establishing missions and building schools.

The third objective eluded him until, by chance, he ventured north aboard the United States Revenue cutter *Bear* to visit some outlying Inuit in 1890. M. A. Healy, the hard-drinking, rugged captain of the *Bear*, brought Jackson's attention to Saint Lawrence Island as they cruised by it one hundred miles southwest of Alaska's Seward Peninsula. Healy told him the island had been devastated by a famine which had snuffed out the lives of most of the inhabitants. He was of the opinion that the solution to such tragedies could be found in Siberia, directly across the Bering Strait from Alaska. The captain pointed out to Jackson that the Siberian natives ran tame reindeer which, unlike their wild cousins, the caribou, could be husbanded like cattle. Thus, they avoided the cycles of feast and famine experienced by caribou hunters.

Jackson immediately saw the value of a domesticated animal that could survive on the tundra, and became convinced that reindeer were the answer to the food crises experienced by the indigenous Alaskans. Employing his clout as the General Education Agent, Jackson ordered a range reconnaissance behind Port Clarence on the Seward Peninsula, the closest natural harbour to Siberia. Ample food plants were found on the tundra and 191 deer were purchased from Siberian Eskimos and landed at Port Clarence in 1892. Four Siberians were brought along to care for the deer and to instruct local residents in how to herd them. However, the four did not fit in, and were replaced by six Laplanders who were brought in from northern Norway.

Jackson's reindeer mission received a boost — and international headlines — when several mining camps in the Yukon were threatened with starvation during the fabled Klondike gold rush. A herd of 538 deer was purchased in Norway and shipped, along with 118 Lapp herders and their families, half way around the world in 1898. The rumoured mass starvation turned out to be less imminent than supposed and half of the reindeer were re-routed to Unalakleet, an Eskimo village on the Seward Peninsula in Alaska. A total of 1,200 reindeer were purchased in Siberia before the Czar halted shipments in 1902. Included in this number were 254 of a larger strain called *Tunguse* purchased from the Russians in the Okhotsk area near the Tunguse mountains of south central Siberia. Special arrangements had been made by the United States government to obtain the Tunguse deer in 1901 in order to increase the size of deer already landed in Alaska by breeding-in the larger strain.

After the long sea voyage from the east coast of central Siberia, the deer arrived at Port Clarence, Alaska in poor condition, barely having survived the tumultuous trip. These deer appeared to be of little value when seen for the first time by the handlers who unloaded them. Their North American sojourn would have implications, however, several decades later when the Canadian government was looking for reindeer.

The number of reindeer in Alaska, after the modest inception of the 1890s and early 1900s, rocketed to dizzying heights by the mid-twenties. Commencing with the original stock, the reindeer population had grown from the first born, *April Fool,* to number a respectable 350,000 by 1925. No less than 110 herds were nestled along the Bering Sea and the Arctic Ocean, employing, through various services, 600 Inuit and several hundred Laplanders. From 1918 to 1925, more than two million pounds of deer meat were sent from Alaska to the United States mainland. Escalation of sales was even more impressive as shipments from the Territory jumped from 200,000 pounds in 1923 to almost 700,000 pounds only two years later.

Cattlemen in mainland United States became worried about inroads of deer meat into their market. On one occasion boycotts were instituted in Kansas and Nebraska when farmers learned that two train carloads of reindeer cuts had been shipped to grocery wholesalers in those states.

The sale of meat brought in a modest flow of cash which filtered down to the herders through the middle men and gave the Inuit a means of exchange. Raising reindeer not only provided the native people with such needs as a permanent food source, but also allowed them a way of accruing cash to purchase goods they could no longer do without, such as rifle cartridges. The fledgling industry at least presented the Inuit a chance to avoid complete dependency on the government.

A reindeer herd has substantial procreative capacities: it will double in size every three years under ideal conditions. If a native sat down and figured it out, the statistics were mind-boggling. If he cultivated a herd for fifteen years, 100 deer could increase to 3,200, or at the going rate of ten dollars a head, a value of $32,000. On the basis of the 1929 economy, the cost of production for each animal was a dollar per year!

The most important aspect in regard to the budding industry was the growth of native Alaskan ownership over the first quarter of a century. By

1925, approximately 175,000 deer had been harvested by the Eskimos for food and by-products, yet the number of deer owned by natives had increased to 200,000. In other words, no matter how one looked at it, the reindeer program was a success, if for no other reason than for the food it provided.

For an outside observer from a country with a disadvantaged native population, this one fact alone would be appealing. Canadian officials were aware of Alaska's success with reindeer, and viewed the industry as a possible answer to recurring problems of starvation among the residents of its northern climes. As early as 1919, a Royal Commission on Muskox and Reindeer[2] had been appointed to investigate the possibilities of establishing a reindeer industry in the Canadian Arctic. Thirty-five persons, most of whom were individuals with polar experience, had appeared before the Commission and testified that the caribou population, upon which some of the native tribes were heavily dependent, was so depleted in many northern areas that the people were literally starving to death.

The Reverend W. G. Walton, a missionary with the Church of England, filed a report with the Commission on May 24, 1920 which was typical of many such treatises emanating from the far-flung north. He tabulated some of the more celebrated encounters with famine: in the Ungava area, 150 Indians died of starvation during the winter of 1892–3 south of Fort Chimo. That same winter seven of eight Indians on a hunting expedition near Cape Jones perished, the lone survivor having resorted to the gruesome option of living off the bodies of the others. During the winter of 1911–12 an Eskimo woman and her two children died of starvation eighty miles north of the Great Whale River trading post. Eleven Indians starved to death in 1918–19 at Richmond Gulf. Yet another three died that year of malnutrition inland from the Great Whale River, and nine more died near Fort George. That winter proved to be one of the worst on record, owing to the scarcity of all wild game.

Viewed from the security of an armchair, starvation invokes visions that inspire sympathy. However, such visions are blurred and devoid of impact when read merely as statistics. Personalizing it, we are presented with a more precise conception of the agony in human terms. Peter Freuchen, one of the Arctic's great explorers, recorded the boyhood experience of an Inuit during a period which the old native described as "The Great Want".[3]

One summer the ice failed to break up, creating, in effect, a two-year-long winter. Game was scarce. The boy's father's hunting partner died and the widow moved in with the child's mother, who was her sister. The lad, who was then in his early teens, had assumed the responsibility of helping his father support the two women and their two children, as well as an elder woman. During the long periods of time his father was gone, hunger gnawed at the vitals of the women and children at home.

Several times the boy saw the women head for a burial plot with knives in hand, though he did not see what they did. The youngest child died and it became apparent they all would die if something was not found to eat.

One night the lad, pretending to sleep, heard one woman whisper to another and point to his foster sister, saying she was strong and fat. He knew they would attempt to kill her, and probably himself, if the situation was right.

The boy thought long and hard that night. He figured if his foster sister and he must die, they might as well die alone, facing the unknowns of the snow and ice, rather than certain death at the hands of the women. He told his foster sister of his plan of escape, but it could not be carried out right away because they had eaten the soles of their shoes and she would have to sew others. Finally that was done, and the boy convinced the other women that he would need his foster sister to help him hunt seals. The two then fled inland. The first day the boy managed to shoot one fox which itself was just skin and bones. The next day their total meal was one ptarmigan, which, as with the fox, they ate raw: without fat to render into fuel, they had no fire. The only way they obtained moisture was to eat snow and ice, which severely burned their lips and mouths.

One can sense the pell-mell advance toward death once the primary necessities of life were denied. Without water, dehydration sets in; without food the muscles commence to deteriorate; and without heat, the inner core of the body cools down and before long the entire organism ceases operating. One deficiency triggers another in rapid succession. The blood pressure drops, the pulse slows down, and the extremities begin to freeze. The skin becomes thin, dry, inelastic, pale and cold. A patchy brown pigmentation may colour the affected parts. The hair becomes dry and sparse and falls out easily. The brain is also affected. Lassitude and apathy make it difficult to focus one's efforts. Irritability is common. Though the intellect may remain clear, the capacity for work is reduced. The colder the temperature, the quicker nature accomplishes its gruesome task, and once weight loss reaches fifty per cent, death is inevitable.

The third day on the move, the two youths had reached the point of no return. They were staggering from weakness. The boy wanted to shoot a dog they had brought along with them, but the girl asked him to wait. Then, suddenly, their fortune turned when the dog scented a bear which the boy tracked to its lair, flushed out, and killed. The siblings rendered the bear's fat into oil, and got a fire going. They entertained thoughts of taking meat back to the women, but they were too weak to accomplish the task and figured the women would be dead anyway. They continued on, eventually met up with another band, and were taken in.

Later the story of the women's fate came out: all had been found dead. The two younger women were discovered with crushed skulls and all of the meat eaten off their bones. Only the older woman's body was whole, though she was emaciated.

Starvation is insidious because of the terrible option which has presented itself hundreds of thousands of times to countless groups of humans inhabiting the vast northland — a macabre choice to devour one's kin or to die.

The Royal Commission's hearings in 1919 sparked interest in reindeer, much of it generated by one of the Commission's four members, Vilhjalmur Stefansson, who resigned when it became apparent there was a conflict of interest between the Commission's requirement for impartiality and his own attempts to establish a reindeer herd in the Canadian Arctic. An early attempt, with the backing of the Hudson's Bay Company, to set up a herd on Baffin Island had failed due to poor planning, but "Stef" remained convinced that viable herds could be set up in the pasturage available around the Mackenzie River delta.

Paradoxically, no one was starving in the Mackenzie delta at the time of Stefansson's recommendation. In fact, of all the places in the Arctic where the people were least likely to starve, the bountiful delta would have been it. The Mackenzie Inuit in historical times numbered around 2,200 people who subsisted chiefly on creatures of the sea, and of the barren lands and forests in the areas of the Kugaluk and Anderson rivers, and the sprawling delta of the Mackenzie River. Caribou, moose and muskox were taken on land, and walrus, seals, and beluga whales were the primary animals taken from the sea.

Kittigazuit, with one thousand inhabitants, was the largest community in the western Arctic. For such a large cluster of nomadic hunters to be present in one place, there had to be an unusually large population of wildlife. And in the delta, the principal source of food were the beluga whales. Weighing up to a ton each, these animals were hunted in a sea version of the simple roundup method of harvesting.[4]

Spokesman for the Canadian government in the North at the time of the Commission was Oswald S. Finnie, a lean, well-groomed individual, who had been director of the Northwest Territories and Yukon Branch of Canada's Department of the Interior for five years. Born in Ontario in 1876, Finnie graduated with a degree in civil and mining engineering from McGill University in 1897. Immediately afterwards he journeyed to Dawson City in the midst of the Yukon gold rush, where he joined the staff of William Ogilvie, Commissioner of the newly formed Yukon Territory. His portfolio included service as the mining recorder and manager of the government office.

Conflicts over mining claims at the height of the gold rush taxed to the limit the patience of civil servants like Oswald Finnie. That he satisfactorily carried out his duties for eleven years under the intense pressure of Dawson City was not lost upon his superiors in Ottawa. When the federal government created the Northwest Territories and Yukon Branch to deal exclusively with the North in 1920, Finnie became its first director. Consequently, when the Royal Commission on Muskox and Reindeer finally issued its recommendations in 1925, they fell squarely within his terms of reference.

Having been in the sub-Arctic and Arctic for most of his working life, Finnie was knowledgeable of the North's many perplexing problems, not the least of which was the ever present scourge of famine. He was convinced the situation was serious enough to warrant initiation of some sort of program that would provide a permanent source of sustenance for the natives.

Another ardent supporter of this concept was lecturer and free-lance writer Henry Toke Munn, who had lived as a trader among the natives of northern Canada for eleven years. In an article which appeared in the Toronto *Star Weekly* in June, 1923, he cited Alaska's success as something the Canadian government should strive to emulate.

The retired trader argued that the Canadian government was the ideal entity by which to introduce reindeer to Canada because it alone could enforce regulations deemed necessary to preserve the herds, while at the same time instructing natives on how to care for the animals. Toke Munn envisioned development of Canada's vast northern prairies (tundra) which he claimed were absolutely worthless for any other agricultural purposes.

Another delegate who supported the concept was Dr. Knud Rasmussen, a member of the Advisory Board of Wildlife Protection of Canada's Department of the Interior. He was a trained ethnologist, and part Eskimo. He had lived among his people and could speak the Inuit dialect. Thus, he possessed the twin advantages of scientific observation and compassion for the Eskimo way of life. His comments carried considerable weight.

"I believe," Rasmussen said, "the introduction of reindeer where there are no caribou would be beneficial and would provide food for the Eskimos. . . ." However, he was not without his reservations. "It will take quite a few years before you can bring enough animals into the country and teach the natives to herd them. I do not believe that herding will be taught in less than a generation," he added.[5]

Such supportive material presented Finnie with the impetus to ask Canada's Department of External Affairs to inquire in the United States as to where the government could purchase such a herd. External Affairs, after an extensive search, came up with the name of a certain Lomen and Company of Nome, Seattle, and New York, a large holder of reindeer herds in Alaska.

CHAPTER 2

A Potential Solution

Lomen and Company, through a daring advertising program promulgated in the United States, was the firm primarily responsible for the boom in the marketing of reindeer meat from 1918 to 1925. Five brothers — Carl, Ralph, George, Alfred, and Harry — had created the company, and named their father, G. J. Lomen, president.

The Lomen brothers were risk takers by inheritance. Their father had walked away from a twenty-year-old law practice in Minneapolis, Minnesota, to join his son Carl in the gold rush to Nome in 1900. Here, the elder Lomen opened another law office. The rest of the family joined G. J. and Carl, and by 1906 the clan had managed to pool their resources to purchase several businesses in the Alaska city.

The Lomens' interest in reindeer operations derived originally from exposure to the herds around Nome, and from Carl's friendship with Walter Shields, who had taken over as chief of the reindeer program by way of his appointment as Superintendent of the Bureau of Education for the Northwest District of Alaska (Sheldon Jackson's former position), under which the project was supported. Shields, though a newcomer from Washington, D. C., saw the vast potential of the industry and strived to impress natives and whites alike with the versatility of reindeer by using them to the exclusion of dogs, for winter travel. In this way he sought to emphasize their value as draft animals.

Carl Lomen accompanied the enthusiastic Shields on five extensive trips through the reindeer camps, and to several of the annual reindeer fairs which Shields had initiated for the purpose of engendering interest in the industry. The "reindeer rodeos" featured competitive events and activities associated with herding deer (lassoing, races, tests of strength) and provided a forum for the herders to swap ideas and information.

In 1912 Superintendent Shields suggested that Carl and his brothers purchase a herd that happened to be up for sale, pointing out that entrepreneurs could play an important role in developing the industry through investment of capital sorely needed for further expansion of the business.

The herd belonged to a man named Alfred Nilima. Nilima had been among the group that sailed from Norway on their purported rescue mission to the Klondike gold miners back in 1898. When the herd was split, Nilima had gone to Unalakleet where he watched a herd on contract for the government. As payment for this service he had been offered an option by which he took the Tunguse deer landed at Port Clarence — which no one else wanted because of their deplorable condition — and drove the herd north to Buckland, fifty miles south of Kotzebue. There he had nurtured the herd for twelve years. Now the Lapp was offering for sale the entire lot, which numbered twelve hundred reindeer, at a price of thirty thousand dollars. The Lomens were game. They offered to take an option on the deer for five thousand down, with the balance to be paid in two equal installments over a period of two years.

Nilima accepted the offer, and in order to finalize the deal, Alfred Lomen crammed five thousand dollars worth of currency into a money belt and hiked several hundred miles to give the Lapp the down payment. When he offered Nilima the money, the herdsman told him he wanted a cheque rather than cash. Lomen, obliging, wrote out a draft on a wallet-worn facsimile, and gave it to the herder. The placid, methodical Lapp finally cashed the note two years later.

Stuck with the greenbacks, Alfred Lomen walked to the coastal town of Candle where he gave the cash to a sea captain and asked him to deliver it to his brothers in Nome. That he had never seen the captain before did not help Alfred's peace of mind any, yet in due course the money was delivered.

The Lomen family sought investors to participate in a corporation they formed to underwrite the cost of the reindeer purchase. The most affluent of the creditors engaged was Jafet Lindeberg, who was the president of the Pioneer Mining and Ditch Company, Nome's largest gold-dredging concern. Lindeberg's interest in the reindeer proposal arose from the fact he had come as foreman from Norway on the same expedition as Nilima. After delivering the deer to Unalakleet, Lindeberg and two partners struck a bonanza on the Snake River, not far from Nome's present location, and had gone on to prosper.

Having acquired the deer, the company now needed a foreman to run the herd and teach the new owners the business. The Lomens selected Andrew Bahr, yet another veteran herder who had journeyed to Alaska under the same contract as Lindeberg and Nilima. His desire, too, had been to prospect for gold rather than to herd reindeer.

Bahr had actually reached the Klondike while escorting the half of the deer herd that had *not* been diverted when the relief expedition was suspended. Released from the reindeer contract, he set out down the Yukon River in pursuit of his dream, but met with a minor disaster when the raft on which he was travelling tipped over in the river and he lost most of his gear. Bahr shrugged off his yearnings for gold and headed for Unalakleet to seek a job with the reindeer.

The Lapp was given a contract by the United States Bureau of Education to watch a small herd for six months. Bureau personnel mislaid instructions for his relief and six *more* months elapsed before they discovered the oversight. An expedition was quickly dispatched to search for Bahr who, to the Bureau's relief, was still at his post watching the animals. The deer were in good condition though they had been buffeted by a series of winter storms. Bahr's dedication and general professionalism made a strong impression on his employers, and from that time onward, he was adjudged one of the most dependable herders in the business.

After purchasing Nilima's herd, the Lomens propitiously decided to concentrate solely on sales in the "Lower 48", the United States mainland, and to leave the local economy to the Eskimos. With Bahr as head herdsman, the company expanded its operations, adding to the herd and hiring more employees, all of them either Lapps or Eskimos.

In 1921, the company suffered a setback when their principal backer, Lindeberg, found it necessary to withdraw his support for the reindeer venture. As a consequence, Carl Lomen left for New York to seek financing, now badly needed if the company was going to continue its expansion. Lomen was able to obtain references from an old acquaintance, Vilhjalmur Stefansson, whom he had known in Nome. After a series of near-misses scouring Wall Street for several hundred-thousand dollars worth of financing Lomen managed to secure the backing of two foresighted attorneys in the prestigious firm of Griggs, Baldwin, and Baldwin.

The Lomen brothers and the Baldwins blended very well. The latter were from upstate New York, where they had been raised on a poverty-ridden dairy farm, which Arthur propounded had been the poorest in the state. One of their first business ventures as youths was selling a skunk pelt for ninety cents, which they split between them. Nevertheless, after graduation from Cornell Law School, they had gone on to set up a highly successful law practice in New York City in partnership with James W. Griggs, former Attorney General of the United States. Their firm represented such notables as Charles W. Murphy when that Irishman was head of the formidable Tammany Hall political machine and the unchallenged boss of New York. Arthur Baldwin was the individual who brought together McGraw and Hill to form the giant publishing firm of the same name. When it came to clout, the Baldwins had plenty of it.

The combination of the Baldwins' influence and the Lomens' enthusiasm was to put the reindeer operation on the crest of a wave of publicity sorely needed to advertise the product. This was exemplified by a "Reindeer Week" celebration they promoted in the mid-twenties. Jimmie Walker, New York City's vibrant mayor, was enlisted by the

Baldwins to proclaim the seven-day festival. The theme of the week was to inform the public that reindeer meat was now available at local butcher shops. Such celebrities as Stefansson; Roald Amundsen, the first man to reach the South Pole; W. C. Henderson of the United States Department of Agriculture; and nationally known food expert, Alfred W. McCann, were enlisted in the campaign.

McCann wrote a column that appeared regularly in the Brooklyn *Daily Times*, where he expressed his appreciation of the fact that reindeer cuts could now be purchased in the city's butcher shops, as well as aboard the crack trains of the Northern, the Soo, Northern Pacific, and Milwaukee railroads. Commenting on the taste of the steaks, McCann wrote: "The flavor of reindeer meat offers not the slightest suggestion of gaminess or wild animal flavor. The meat is finer in texture than beef and far more tender. It has all the juiciness of beef with the texture of lamb, but tastes like neither. It is actually delicate in flavor."[1]

Thanks to New York's media, Reindeer Week was successful in acquainting gourmets with a new dimension in the culinary field. Such promotions served to make Lomen and Company synonymous with the reindeer industry. It followed that anyone interested in raising reindeer would do well to seek out the Lomens. Canada's External Affairs Department had done this when they contacted Leonard Baldwin in New York City on behalf of Oswald Finnie.

Leonard Baldwin responded to the Canadian request by sending O. S. Finnie a booklet describing the reindeer program. At the same time, he asked the director if he could render any assistance on the subject.

Finnie replied on August 22, 1925 outlining his needs: "If it were possible to transport reindeer from Alaska . . . it seems to me this would be the salvation of these (Eskimo) people." He added: "Perhaps you could give us an idea of what it might cost to herd, say, two thousand reindeer, leaving them in two herds — one in the neighborhood of the Mackenzie River, on the east side thereof, and the other in the vicinity of the Anderson or Horton River."[2]

After conferring with Carl Lomen in Seattle, Baldwin advised Finnie the Lomen Company could do the job. He said their company could deliver the deer to the east side of the Mackenzie for $150 a head. He added they would do it for $25 a head less if delivered to the west side. The company would require a quarter of the total sum as down payment, and six months' notice to prepare for the expedition.

Finnie, who did not pretend to be any sort of an expert on reindeer, forwarded Baldwin's letter to Maxwell Graham of the Wildlife Branch of Canada's Department of the Interior, for his opinion. Graham responded with several objections, one to the price and the other to the suggestion of delivery west of the river. He cited the fact that the Hudson's

Bay Company, in its venture, had purchased deer delivered from Norway for $65 a head. He felt that $75 would be more acceptable. At this point, both parties were postulating about the price; such a drive had never been attempted before, so estimates of cost were only an educated guess. Naturally the purchaser was on the low side, with the seller the opposite.

Finnie capsulized Graham's observations and sent them to Baldwin, reiterating that he was more interested in having the deer delivered to the *east* bank. The latter point highlighted one stumbling block for deer driven from Alaska; the Mackenzie could not be approached from the west without going through a thirty-mile tangle of willows, alders, and buckbrush where the tundra of the Arctic coast met the tree line of the river delta. Because this morass was impassable, the herd would have to be driven in mid-winter right out onto the bay where the river flows into the Arctic Ocean. This island-splayed sound was eighty miles across, and contained a twenty-mile-wide stretch of open ice. The deer, without food as an enticement to hold them, would be extremely susceptible to stampeding if hit by a storm during the crossing.

In the meantime, the Lomens moderated their asking price. The company would reduce the price per head to $75 for deer delivered to the west side of the river if 3,000 were purchased. Again, Finnie forwarded the terms to Graham, who saw them as more realistic, but he still objected to the place of delivery.

At this point, Finnie's superior, Deputy Minister of the Department of the Interior, W. W. Cory, advised him to defer negotiations until a proper study could be made of the grazing land in the delta area. Haggling over the price of the herd's delivery would be a waste of time if the region could not support any reindeer in the first place.

Cory was an attorney; thus he and Finnie, who was an engineer, constituted a good, pragmatic team to launch the reindeer project. Though eleven years older than Finnie, Cory had joined the Interior Department three years after his colleague, first serving in the Dominion Lands Department. He spent four summers in Dawson City, from 1901 to 1903, where the two had come to know each other well. In 1904, Cory had been named Assistant Commissioner of the Lands Department, and the following year was promoted to the Deputy Minister position.

Finnie and Cory had worked together for twenty-five years by 1925, and in the course of that time had travelled extensively throughout the Arctic, evaluating its needs. And though optimistic about the North's future, they were prudent enough to proceed with caution when it came to grandiose schemes concerning economic development. They knew the one thing a man learned in the Arctic and sub-Arctic — and that was to exercise patience in the face of the formidable odds Nature had dealt in the implacable northland.

The two administrators agreed that an expert from the scientific community, ideally a botanist, would have to be found to take on the job of surveying the feasibility of the reindeer project. This would have to be done before the Canadian parliament could be asked to fund the program. A salary was allotted for such a position, which for budgetary reasons was labelled an "Exploratory Engineer". The pay was set at $2,700 a year with an additional $1,500 provided for a living allowance, and another $800 for expenses. Finnie suggested an assistant's position be added, as the botanist would be called on to travel long distances over the tundra, and under such circumstances could not be expected to go alone because of the risks involved. An allotment was set aside for this position as well.

Cory queried the chief of the United States Biological Survey, E. W. Nelson, for information about reindeer operations in Alaska while Finnie circulated a memo through different departments of government to see if a botanist could be obtained from one of them. Announcements were also sent to the major universities in the nation. The response to the Canadian government's request for a botanist was not overwhelming, and what few applications did come in were not acceptable. Ultimately, A. Erling Porsild was suggested for the position. He was the son of a Danish professor of botany who had set up a botanical research station in

Disko Island off the west coast of Greenland in 1906. Young Porsild had lived most of his life in this bleak environment, spoke fluent Eskimo, and had handled dog teams since he was a youth. He had eventually earned a Degree in Botany from the University of Copenhagen. His older brother, Thor, who later preferred to be called Bob, had attended the same school to study biology, and was obviously a candidate for the assistant's job. Bob had been raised in the same environment, and had a repertoire of skills learned from the hard lessons of experience. He spoke passing Inuit, could forge a sled, had hunted seals and polar bear, could build a snow shelter, and above all, like his brother he possessed the scientific knowledge to go along with his other qualifications. Equally important, Bob and Erling were in their twenties, young and physically strong.

In addition, a strict, no-nonsense martinet of a father had honed them to be as tough mentally as they were physically. When they were told to do something, they did it, and they did it right. Bob was bigger and stronger physically than Erling, the latter having had a bout with tuberculosis that was cured by his mother's insistence he return to Disko Island from Denmark, where he had been in University. Erling, on the other hand, held the edge in power of will. Nothing, but nothing, could deter Erling when his mind was set on a course of action. Bob was more conciliatory and compromising than was his younger brother.

Deputy Minister Cory, when advised of the availability of Erling Porsild by M. O. Malte, chief botanist for the United States National Herbarium, contacted the younger Porsild in the state of Illinois, where the scientist was pursuing advanced studies at the University of Chicago. Cory entrained to the Windy City and was so impressed by the young Dane's qualifications that, after further consultations with Nelson in Washington, he hired both Erling and Bob, in May 1926. The deputy minister summarized his expectations of what the Porsilds were to accomplish: They were to study the myriad complexities of the reindeer industry in Alaska and learn the main principles fundamental to success. Those principles would then be applied to determine the viability of introducing the deer into northwestern Canada. The final word on the subject was dependent on their recommendations: if Erling Porsild concluded that the project was not feasible, Finnie would shelve it.

Erling and Bob were of a kind, with a proper respect for the Arctic environment, a youthful enthusiasm, and a vast capacity for learning. Nelson of the U. S. Biological Survey made arrangements to show them around Alaska, suggesting that Erling and Bob observe a number of different herds, beginning that August, in order to see the practical applications of grazing techniques. This meant attending roundups as well, where they would learn how to capture, corral, and care for the deer. They studied the methods of notching the deer's ears to prove ownership; Arctic conditions and the deer's peculiar skin made branding impractical.

The Porsilds were taught that deer, like people, have their own idiosyncrasies. Reindeer will mill (circle) when agitated, either one way or the other in a corral, but not both ways. In other words, if a particular herd circles clockwise, it will never go in the opposite direction. Therefore a herder wanted to make sure the ears of the reindeer were marked on the side that could be seen from the fence. Even the structure of the corral depended on the direction the deer milled. Funnel-shaped holding-pens inside the corral were built with their wide end facing the direction of milling, so that the deer would naturally run *into* the separating pens, rather than sweep by the opening, missing it. The tendency to mill is the clue to another typical difficulty in working reindeer — once they are disturbed, it is difficult to calm them down again.

Erling and Bob viewed one of the preferred corral designs at the Buckland camp. The compound was circular and exceptionally large, so that the heat from the bodies of the tightly packed deer would not melt the surface snow, which might then later freeze to an icy glaze. The secret to the success of this type of paddock was the construction of separating pens, or pockets, located on either side of the exit from the main corral to the chute through which the animals passed individually to be treated. These pens allowed the herd to be divided into small bunches and put through the chutes as needed, thus avoiding the old method of lassoing each deer for de-horning, castrating, or to examine them for ownership, disease, or other purposes.

Other elements of corralling learned from the hard voice of experience were passed on to the Porsilds. If, for example, reindeer were processed too slowly, deer held outside the corral could decimate the forage by undue trampling. In addition, the ground would become contaminated with excrement and a magnet for parasites.

Starvation was always a possibility if the deer overgrazed the surrounding tundra. There were no feasible ways of importing food from neighbouring regions as could be done in cattle-raising areas. For this reason portable corrals were designed. They could be moved periodically, thus controlling the area in which the deer fed and affording the deer a bountiful food supply without destroying the tundra.

Herdsmen were quick to point out to the two Danes that a grazing range might be appropriate in the summer, but vagaries of climate could make the same area a death trap for deer at other times of the year. Coastal areas were acceptable locales in the warm months because ocean breezes kept warble flies and mosquitoes at bay. However, in winter, these places were susceptible to chinooks which blew in warm air, bringing rain and unseasonal thaws. If the ensuing carpet of water froze to a deep enough thickness, the deer would starve to death because they could not paw through the ice to feed on the lichens trapped underneath.

Such conditions demanded that the deer be moved to higher ground in order to avoid the ice problem. But herding in interior pastures had drawbacks as well. Deprived of an access to the sea coast, the deer's only means of escape from insects was on the higher mountain tops. If there were no mountains high enough and sufficiently exposed to cool breezes, that region was considered a poor one in which to run deer.

Erling and Bob learned that reindeer, though they resemble cattle on the range, actually banded together like sheep. They were also similar to horses in that they nervously trampled the range, grazing as they went; but unlike horses, they travelled against the wind rather than with it.

One of the biggest problems of management arose from the deer's homing instinct. In open-range country as found in Alaska, where natural barriers were relatively few (though still more than in Canada's northwest), this gave rise to all sorts of disputes and charges, not the least of which was rustling. Often, when reindeer were sold or transferred from one herd to another, the animals would return to their former owner, sometimes passing through and drawing off animals from other herds along the way.

Yet another problem involved the social aspects

of a reindeer's nature. Inevitably, they were attracted to a larger group. Thus, if a large caribou herd migrated through an area, deer in a smaller group would drift off with it.

It seemed every time Erling and Bob turned around they discovered something new. Erling summed up his observations when he wrote: "Even if we have not gained the skill of trained reindeer men, we have learned enough to ascertain for ourselves if a herd is handled correctly and efficiently or not."[3]

The brothers finally wound up their investigations at Kotzebue, and in December 1926 plotted their route to the Mackenzie delta for the next phase of their study. The path would take them along the northwest coast of Alaska to Barrow, then along the shores of the Arctic Ocean across the Yukon Territory to Aklavik, in Canada's Northwest Territories. The route along the coastline, though a little longer than a direct overland route, would avoid the interior mountains and keep them closer to coastal settlements. Erling felt this trip would also afford them an excellent opportunity to study reindeer herders in another environment, that of the Arctic coast where there were few white men. The Eskimos' prosperity in this region — or lack of it — would give the Porsilds a good indication of how feasible the concept of herding reindeer would be in Canada. Another objective of their scouting was to search for forage that would sustain a large herd on a trail drive. Winter forage consisted of various mosses such as heath, pad, reindeer, fern, bunch, and Iceland. Berries such as the mountain cranberry also lay frozen under the snow. Summer plants they would search for included willows, birch, vetch, dock, gentian, blueberry, crowberry, and such grasses as water buttercup and fern weed.

The Porsilds' trip back to Canada was itself an accomplishment of major proportions, mushing through fifteen hundred miles of some of the most inhospitable land on earth. Barely a week out on the trail, the two brothers rounded Cape Beaufort only to be walloped by a blizzard from the far reaches of Siberia. The men managed to find refuge in an Eskimo pit-cabin already occupied by four native families numbering fifteen people. They bivouacked here for ten long days. The unintentional roommates were soon relegated to eating fish the scientists had brought along to feed their dogs. Four of Bob's animals and one of Erling's died of starvation and exposure.

Several weeks later, after reaching Beechey Point, the dogs again exhausted to the point of uselessness, the two men decided Erling should continue eastward alone leaving Bob to catch up whenever he felt his dogs were fit enough to travel.

Even under ideal conditions, to make a solitary journey through one of the most treacherous areas of the globe as Erling was about to do tempted fate to the utmost. Almost any unexpected mishap, however apparently minor at first, could endanger a wayfarer's life. If a man fell off his sled and missed grabbing on to the safety line that normally trailed behind, there was the chance his dogs would keep running and disappear in the distance, possibly attracted by the enticing whiff of caribou from an offshore wind. Thus stranded, the musher might die of exposure, starvation or a combination of the two. Even *with* his team there was always the possibility of the musher falling into an open lead of water, or of breaking an ankle, or of wrenching a knee, or of experiencing any number of ailments such as influenza, that could render him incapable of continuing or extricating himself from his predicament.

Erling travelled safely across the Yukon–Alaska border, but soon after, the botanist found out that he was not immune to mishaps. In hefting the heavy sled after the half-ton load had tipped over, he wrenched a groin muscle, and by the time he reached Herschel Island two days later, he was in intense pain from a hernia. As a result, the police inspector at Herschel detailed a constable to take him the rest of the way to Aklavik, where Porsild arrived April 9, 1927. His brother reached the delta community a week later, completing a trip few explorers could have achieved as competently.

The journey left the Porsilds with a nagging worry over the efficiency of Inuit herders because of sloppy techniques they spotted. Of one Erling wrote: "He himself, when his herd was not doing well, at once lost interest in it and though he was known as a very good reindeer man before, the herd suffered sadly from mismanagement."[4] This herder's case was not unique, and the same scenario was repeated again and again in Alaska. Erling stressed that Eskimos could be good men when under the supervision of a white man, but if left to themselves they tended to neglect the herd when increases in the number of animals, and profits, were not up to expectations.

All the blame, however, was not laid on the Eskimos. Erling cited the fact that white fox furs were selling at a premium, and consequently, pursuit of the furs caused them to neglect the deer.[5]

These evaluations were to be of extreme importance relative to the ultimate recommendations Erling would make on whether or not a reindeer herd should be initiated in Canada. As far as he was concerned, it would be all right to help the Inuit, but if the native people were reluctant to assume the burden and responsibility of managing a herd of deer, some other arrangement would have to be made, such as hiring Lapps, pending a change of attitude. Otherwise, the program would have to be nixed altogether.

After a few months' rest, the brothers set out again in July 1927 to accomplish the formidable task of examining the prospective range lands of the Mackenzie delta. Travelling by gas boat, they went as far east as the Anderson River, north to Richards Island, and south to Eskimo Lakes.

Their research revealed the forage in the area to be viable and actually better for sustaining reindeer than much of the range in use by herders in Alaska. According to the estimates of the Porsilds, the area that included Richards Island and the mainland was capable of supporting 250,000 reindeer.

Erling wired their findings to Finnie at the conclusion of the trip in September 1927. His message read: "Returned east eleventh instant having completed . . . traverse approximately 15,000 square miles of reindeer pasture ranging in every respect with best types found in Alaska."[6]

When Finnie received the telegram, he sent a note to representatives of the American government, and to Deputy Minister Cory, advising them of the optimistic statement on the grazing potential. Perhaps a deal could be struck after all.

Erling Porsild's terms of reference required that he carry out additional range reconnaissance. In December, he and his brother made a quick trip by dog team to investigate winter grazing conditions over the same area they had covered that summer. Returning in January 1928, they rested for a month, and then launched another dog-sled trip to check out winter grazing conditions that took them as far east as Great Bear Lake. They concluded this journey in time to catch the last boat up the Mackenzie River in September 1928, and reached Ottawa soon afterwards.

Erling then filed his formal report. In it, he took pains to advise Finnie of the many problems which could arise in respect to establishing a reindeer industry in northwestern Canada. He recommended where to purchase range stock, routes the proposed reindeer drive should take, the type of facilities needed to receive the deer, and a variety of other details that would have to be included in any contract negotiated for purchasing the deer.

Erling enumerated four basic requirements that would have to be fulfilled before any agreement could be signed. These called for: Delivery of the heard *east* of the Mackenzie River *before* fawning season; steers to be accepted only at a much lower price than breeding stock; two experienced reindeer men to stay on with the herd for at least two years; and the prime cost of the deer should be considerably under that of one hundred twenty-five per head sought by the Lomen brothers.

The botanist displayed little confidence in the prospect of letting Canadian Eskimos handle the deer on their own for the first two years. Instead, he opined that besides the two Alaskan herders, two young married Lapps be brought over from Norway to handle the herd. Their services would suffice until the local inhabitants learned how to handle the job.

Porsild attached a proposed cost sheet for initial expenditures which totalled $276,000. Summarizing the potential of the project, he pointed out that the reindeer operation could expect an increase of sixty to seventy-five per cent per year on females, though the actual ratio of males to females at birth was even. Females were to be retained at the same percentage level as their increase. Surplus males would be castrated and eventually killed for meat. Porsild estimated a well-managed herd of three thousand deer could supply five hundred to seven hundred and fifty steers a year for the local market in the Mackenzie delta, which he felt was adequate to absorb the kill, and thus be self-supporting after the first couple of years of operation.

The Porsilds' journey had been reported by the major papers of North America. Newsmen were generally supportive of initiating a reindeer industry in their articles concerning the reindeer venture. The Montreal *Gazette's* editorial of December 19, 1928, was representative of the majority when it wrote: "If success can be achieved after the reindeer have been introduced . . . a new era may be opened up for Canada's northland. A meat industry of great proportions may be developed. . . . "

CHAPTER 3

Preparations

Early in 1929 Erling Porsild penned a memo to Finnie in which he noted that a long interval had passed since the government had been in correspondence with Alaska's reindeer men. He suggested that new quotations be solicited on the price of a herd. Finnie agreed this would be a good idea, and asked for recommendations on those companies that could best supply reindeer.

Porsild's United States contact, L. J. Palmer, recommended the Lomen brothers on the basis of superior herds, better organization, and more encompassing commercial interests in coastal shipping than other ranchers in Alaska. The Lomens also owned several trading posts, as well as a canning plant and a reindeer by-products plant.

The Canadian government, therefore, focused its attention on the Lomen brothers. Erling Porsild gave Deputy Minister Cory a thorough briefing before he entrained for New York to review the final positions of each party. Porsild reiterated that any offer considered by Cory should require the herd to be delivered east of the Mackenzie River. He also advised that the down payment should not be more than twenty-five per cent of the cost. He stressed that a secondary installment be avoided completely "as considerable difficulties are apt to arise on the last part of the drive that may seriously threaten the welfare of the entire herd."[1] By this he meant the crossing of the Mackenzie delta, which was recognized by all parties as a formidable obstacle. In other words, if the Lomens were paid the extra increment and lost the herd on the crossing, the Canadian government would be the loser.

The conference of Cory and Baldwin went off without a hitch in New York City, and the final contract was signed on May 8, 1929. The Canadian government agreed to pay the Lomen Reindeer Corporation a total of $195,000 with $30,000 down on August 1, 1929, another payment of $82,500 a year later (ignoring Porsild's advice), and the balance when three thousand deer were delivered on the east side of the Mackenzie delta. Other "housekeeping" details provided that the drive must be launched on or before October 15, 1929, and that a price of $20 a head be set for all deer delivered in excess of 3,000.

The Lomens agreed to furnish a bond that guaranteed restitution of funds advanced by the government if, for some reason, the herd was not delivered. This clause, and the fact that the wealthy and philanthropic Leonard Baldwin was the guarantor, was one of the principal reasons for Canada choosing the Lomen organization.

Signing of the contract sent both parties into a whirlwind of activity. Finnie dispatched the two Porsild brothers to different destinations: Erling departed for Kotzebue to observe selection of the herd, while Bob was assigned the difficult task of choosing a site for a reindeer station at the final destination. Once that was accomplished, he was to build housing facilities for personnel, and erect corrals and chutes to handle the deer.

While the Porsilds went about their assignments, the Lomen Company put into motion its own plans. Alfred and Carl met with Dan Crowley at their office on the waterfront in Seattle. Dan was a robust man in his fifties, with a wide Irish smile and an easy mien. He had first landed in Alaska in 1900 in search for gold but had had little success in his prospecting venture. He became a merchant in Nome, but left that enterprise when the Lomens offered him the job of field superintendent shortly after they purchased their herd. With regards to the drive, the Lomens decided that Dan should be the communications link between them and the herd's "ramrod," who was yet to be chosen.

The Lomens and Crowley were hard put to select a foreman for the drive. They were in agreement that their choice would have to be either a Lapp or an Eskimo, as men of those two ethnic groups were generally the best qualified by experience. The Lapps particularly possessed the patience needed to successfully complete the reindeer trek. Herding was a tedious business, *especially* with reindeer. To move a herd ten miles was considered an exceptional day. Slow travel and customary twenty-four-hour shifts could make a mental wreck of an inexperienced man in a matter of weeks.

Carl Lomen called a general meeting of former herders — most of them Lapps — who lived in the Seattle area. He sought their advice about the choice of a leader for the drive, and their suggestions as to how the operation could best be carried out. After discussing the various problems that would have to be met, Lomen finally asked the men in attendance who they thought would qualify for the task of leading the drive. After a moment of silence, Andrew Bahr spoke up:

"Why don't you offer me the job?" he asked.

The question came as a shock to Carl Lomen. Though he realized Bahr was a good herder, he also knew the Lapp was at least fifty-five years old, maybe even sixty.

Lomen, on recovering from the impact of Bahr's query, realized that he could do worse. As far as Carl was concerned, no one was better qualified, both mentally and physically, despite the Laplander's age. If Bahr had any weakness, it was in his capacity to lead men. The sometimes taciturn Lapp was more inclined to supervise by example — that is, by just doing it himself — than by force of personality, but his overall demeanour and capabilities were too valuable to ignore. Carl looked around the room to see if there were any frowns from the others present, and seeing none, told Bahr the job was his. Andrew nodded his acceptance.

Bahr had retired after almost twelve years as foreman of the Lomens' herds in Buckland, Alaska in 1926, and had moved to Seattle. He had been thrifty and saved enough money to take advantage of a land boom that swept many areas of the United States at that time by investing in two apartment houses located at the foot of fashionable Queen Anne Hill in Seattle. Bahr also purchased a comfortable home for himself where he lived with his Lapp wife, Marith, and twenty-four-year-old daughter Margaret. Times were prosperous in the United States from 1926 to 1929, and Bahr seemed to be living a life of ease.

Andy Bahr's affection for reindeer herding, however, was not yet out of his blood. Though for three years he had been relatively inactive, he was ripe for such an offer for a number of reasons. He felt he could help his friends, the Eskimos, who were in dire straits on the Canadian side of the line, at least according to most reports he had read in the newspapers. And he figured the money he would make would be a cushion for his own debts on the apartment houses.

Bahr was certainly fit. He exuded health from every pore. His blue eyes danced and twinkled like distant stars, giving evidence of the alert mind that functioned behind them. His face, though lined by years of exposure to the elements, reflected the glow of youth. He was a stocky man, but his tread was soft as a wolf, yet as springy as the deer he had watched over.

The middle-aged Laplander was the epitome of a good reindeer man; he knew the tricks of the trade, and acknowledged that "deer run the herder" rather than the other way around. Honed by half a century outdoors in Norway and Alaska, there was little he did not know about the every-day necessity of being able to survive in the northern wilderness in which he had grown up. Once, when Bahr was caught in a blizzard which cut visibility to less than a yard while he searched for his base camp at Buckland, he suddenly stopped, calculating that he must be near the community. He unhitched the draft deer, tied them to the side of his sled, and went to sleep wrapped in a robe with the storm howling around him. The next morning he awoke to the pealing of the Buckland school bell. Bahr had pegged his sled dead-on in the centre of the village.

Another time, he and an Eskimo lad were trapped by a furious snow storm that seemed to have swept in from nowhere.

"We're lost," the boy cried.

Andrew turned almost haughtily to the youngster and asked, "Can you see me?"

The boy nodded.

"Well," Bahr said, "as long as you can see me, you're as good as home."[2]

Mike Nilluka was selected as second-in-command to Bahr. Mike had been superintendent of a herd owned by the Lomens at Golovin, east of Nome. He was a forthright individual, not known to be the most diplomatic of characters.

With the problem of leadership settled by the selection of the two Lapps, another had to be resolved: the route of the trail drive. Surprising as it seems, even though four years of negotiations had preceded the signing of the contract, the Lomens had not yet settled on the route, though they did know which one they would *not* take. This was the coastal path followed by the Porsilds on their reconnaissance trip, straight north from Kotzebue along the western coast. The Lomens were afraid that Eskimo herds along the coast would be drawn off by the Canada-bound animals. If this happened, they would incur the enmity of the natives. This meant the only alternative was to take an inland route and cross the dreaded spires of the Brooks Range, which spread in a convex crescent, isolating the Arctic Ocean coastal plain from the rest of Alaska. To take a more southerly route was impossible, since that would have meant getting tangled up in the tree line, and in any case, would have taken them too far from potential supply depots on the Arctic coast.

With the help of crude maps they possessed, Alfred and Carl plotted a route from Naboktoolik where the drive would start, to Kittigazuit on the East Channel of the Mackenzie delta. Noting the awesome obstacles that lay in between, the Lomens estimated the drive would have to be undertaken in four stages. First, the deer would have to be driven to the Kobuk River, a short stage to get both deer and herders accustomed to the procedures. Then, across the Brooks Range to the Colville River, almost halfway to their destination. From there the herd would go north-east to the Arctic coast, and finally, the fourth stage would see them along the long stretch to the Mackenzie delta.

Since the maps were vague, the trail boss would have to find his way along as he went, taking advantage of what few identifiable features there were.

The uncertainties of direction, terrain, and the restricted time frame allotted, posed further perplexing riddles for the expedition's planners. How much food, clothes, and camping gear should they allocate when they had only vague notions as to how long the expedition would last?

The Lomens, Bahr, and the Porsild brothers estimated the drive might take from eighteen months to two years, based on some minor moves previously made by herds in Alaska. Yet simple logistics limited them to toting supplies for only a six-month period. After that, food staples would have to be shipped by air, or on trading ships that plied the coast of the Arctic Ocean during the short summer season.

The main task of moving the camp supplies and equipment was to be accomplished by using upwards of twenty to thirty reindeer to pull forty freight sleds. Depending on the load, a deer could pull several sleds in tandem. Since the sleds could be crafted in Seattle, artisans were put to work on them immediately. The sleds were then shipped north as soon as the ice floes had released their grip on the Bering Sea. Carl and Alfred Lomen, along with Dan Crowley, left for Nome on June 5, 1929, and a month later Mike Nilluka and Andrew Bahr sailed north to Kotzebue.

If you look on a map, Kotzebue, Naboktoolik, and the point of intersection of the Hunt and the Kobuk Rivers form the points of an almost equal-sided triangle. The distance from the staging grounds at Naboktoolik to the mouth of the Hunt is slightly longer than the other two arms of the triangle — one hundred miles or so — but was the most direct overland route for the first leg of the drive.

Bahr figured he could save time and hardship by shipping the bulk supplies not needed to begin the drive along another arm of the triangle: direct from Kotzebue via the Kobuk River to its junction with the Hunt. In this way he would avoid the extra work of first relaying material by sled along the third arm (that is, from Kotzebue to Naboktoolik), only to have to take it then along on the first part of the drive. Hiring a boat, he and Nilluka made several trips from Kotzebue up the Kobuk to store provisions in a cache near where the Hunt met it.

The period immediately prior to the scheduled launch of the drive was tense with pressure on Bahr to put the final preparations in place. October 15, 1929 was the announced date the expedition was to move out, but as that departure time approached, it became obvious the herd would not even be rounded up, let alone ready for the trail. There were two reasons for this failure — the weather, and logistical problems. Unseasonal warmth left the boggy tundra unfrozen, making it next to impossible for herders to tramp across it to round up the reindeer. The second reason was that Bahr became overly preoccupied with assembling the cache on the Kobuk with the result that he neglected other aspects of the preparation, and so missed the scheduled departure date.

Canada's representative, Erling Porsild, reached Nome on September 13, but due to poor weather was forced to bide his time in that community for a week prior to flying to the Lomen reindeer camp at Elephant Point. This station was the largest of its kind in Alaska; three different herds were managed from this complex. The reindeer were so numerous and scattered over so wide an area, the Lomens used planes to locate the deer at roundup time. The aircraft saved the firm hundreds of hours that would normally be spent by herders in searching for the animals. Porsild's purpose in visiting Elephant Point was to observe the facilities, and to inspect and approve selection of the reindeer being assembled for the drive.

Bahr finally moved to Naboktoolik at the beginning of November. This camp, situated forty miles straight east from Elephant Point, was not an unfamiliar location to the old Lapp; in fact, he was the one who had originally set it up in 1908 while in the employ of Alfred Nilima as a herder. The name of the place, translated from Inuit, meant "place where there is timber". Though scattered, the timber was a prerequisite in reindeer ranching; it was needed for building corrals, supply and storage sheds, and living quarters, and as a source of fuel.

Lingering uncertainty over exactly which route to take may also have contributed to the postponed starting date, for the details still had not been confirmed. This applied specifically to the paths to be taken across the Schwatka Mountains that divided the Kobuk and Noatak rivers, and farther on, across the Brooks Range from the Noatak to the Colville River.

Bahr and Porsild conferred at Elephant Point and decided to make use of a pilot based there to trace a route across the two formidable land barriers. Frank Dorbandt, flying a Pacific Alaska Airlines plane, took them across the Kobuk delta to the Hunt River, along which they flew looking for a viable pass through the mountains, but the plane was socked-in by bad weather and they returned without verifying a route.

Porsild then accompanied Bahr by dog team to Naboktoolik where Bahr's crew of nine men was just completing enlargement of the corral prior to processing the herd through the chutes. Erling's presence was required under the terms of the contract. It was up to him to ascertain if the deer were healthy, and to make sure the proper ratio of females to males was upheld by the Lomens, though the exact ratio was not stipulated in the contract, but was left to the buyer. Initially, Andrew Bahr had estimated that there were enough deer in the vicinity to provide for the Canadian herd, but by mid-November he realized he was going to come up short. Most of the deer contracted for were to be does, but in actuality the men would have to round up almost twice that many reindeer because males and females each numbered roughly fifty per cent in the uncut herds.

Bahr notified Dan Crowley in Elephant Point of his problem, whereupon Crowley dispatched another herder to drive his animals to Bahr's reindeer camp. They arrived in the last week of November.

No sooner were these deer counted and the animals finally assembled than a vicious storm blew in off the Bering Sea. The onslaught of hurricane-force winds and snow descended on the camp so quickly the herders were barely able to make it to shelter, and were forced to leave the deer to their own devices. The storm ripped apart the corral, and the deer, with the barriers down, fled with the storm, scattering in all directions. They were not rounded up until early December when they again had to be counted through the corral. By the time this was done, the timetable for the commencement of the drive was already two months behind schedule.

The rampant incursions of bad weather bode ill tidings for the drive. Events in another part of the world did nothing to detract from this portent of bad luck.

On October 29 the stock market collapsed in the world's financial capitals. Forever to be known as "Black Tuesday" on the floor of the New York Stock Exchange, this event was to indirectly affect everyone in North America, including the Lomen Company, their employees, and Andy Bahr. The economic nightmare that followed the crash saw prices tumble not only on stocks, but also on such commodities as beef. This forced down the value of deer meat as well, and later threatened the entire industry.

Another disaster, albeit a local one, cast a pall over the drive. Pilot Ben Eielson, president of Pacific Alaska Airlines, and his mechanic, Earl Borland, disappeared on a flight near the Siberian coast while engaged on a contract to transport furs from a ship stranded in the ice pack.[3] The search for Eielson delayed the arrival of W. B. Miller at Naboktoolik. Miller, an assistant to Doctor Palmer at the Fairbanks Experimental Station, had planned to travel with the trail drive while it was in Alaska, to make observations on the mammoth reindeer drive for their own future reference.

Miller was delayed several weeks in Nome because all available planes were involved in the search for the missing men. Ultimately, Miller was able to obtain passage, though he might have been better off walking. His journey graphically illustrated the hardships of air travel at that time: it took Miller seven days to "fly" three hundred miles! During the trip, he and pilot Alger Graham were forced down by weather, ran out of gas once, and finally, crashed on take-off when the landing gear of the plane collapsed. The harried passenger then took to the more traditional mode of travel, a dog team, and mushed the remaining ninety miles to the reindeer camp, arriving there on Christmas Eve, 1929. The short "flight" had rendered him exhausted before he even started out on the drive.

The initial crew picked for the journey was comprised of five Lapp and five Eskimo herders, a physician, Dr. L. E. Benson, and a dog musher hired for the first few days. The observer, Miller, was slated to accompany them for an indefinite period.

The Lapps, besides Bahr and Nilluka, were Andrew Bango, Tom Nakkala, and Ivar West, who had come over to North America in the same expedition as Bahr in 1898. Bango, at twenty, was the youngest, born of Lapp parents in the community of Nulato, Alaska. The Eskimos selected were earnest, hard-working young men in their twenties with experience in all phases of herding reindeer. Three of them, Shelby David, David Henry and August Ome, were from the community of Golovin east of Nome, and the other two, Sam Segeok and Theodore Kingeak, were from the Kotzebue area.

Three of Bahr's crew were well known in a number of cities in mainland United States from having participated in Santa Claus promotions at Christmas. Nilluka had been to Portland, Oregon; Theodore Kingeak to Brooklyn, Newark and Atlanta; and Bango to Philadelphia. The promotions involved local newspapers and department stores and thus served to bring the herders' names before the public.

Bango experienced an amusing incident on one of his trips to the "City of Brotherly Love". He was in charge of several reindeer which a large department store had leased from the Lomen Corporation for a Christmas promotion. A competing merchant brought in animals as well, advertising them as "reindeer". Bango's hosts threatened to sue, claiming the other store was hoodwinking the public because their "reindeer" were really elk. The competitor strategically withdrew the elk.

Wages varied, the inequities of which were to cause problems from the onset. Bahr, as trail boss, was to receive $4,000 a year, Nilluka, Nakkala, and West, classed as "experienced" were to receive $2,400, and Bango, $1,800. The Eskimo herders were all classified in one salary slot at $1,200 per year, $600 less than the lowest Lapp salary.

Allowance for a physician, L. E. Benson, was $4,000 a year, and for a musher and his dog team, $3,000. Notable by its absence was any allocation for a cook.

The vague aspects of distance and time made it

difficult to estimate the need for such items as clothing and food supplies. The variety of simple footwear, for example, reflected the extremes of weather and terrain that Bahr and his men expected to encounter. The Inuit have at least five different words for boots or their parts: *tuttulik* (caribou soles), *ugrulik* (seal soles), *kaglik* (waterproof boots), *paunjaak* (rubber boots) and *kamik* or *mukluk* (caribou-skin boots).

Each man was given two pairs of knee-high fur boots, one pair of ankle-length boots, one pair of seal-skin boots, ten pairs of mukluks, one pair of moccasins, and six pairs of insoles. In addition, the Lapps sometimes used their own style of boots into which they stuffed tundra grass to absorb moisture and thus insure warmth. In seeking adequate footwear, material was required that was at once supple enough for flexing one's toes (to maintain circulation), yet also allowed for evaporation. Mukluks made out of caribou or reindeer skins filled this need, and were irreplaceable in deep, dry snow at forty-below-zero temperatures.

Overflow caused by a rising river, fast-flowing springs that never froze, slush ice, water from hot springs, and unseasonal thaws were conditions that made waterproof foot gear necessary. Sealskin boots were commonly favoured in such emergencies, as against rubber boots in which one's feet sweated, and then were in danger of freezing.

Other clothing was equally important. Lapp and Eskimo women sewed reindeer-skin parkas, fur underwear, and fur pants for the herdsmen. A caribou- or reindeer-skin sleeping bag with a canvas-drill cover provided maximum warmth, and enabled a man to obtain proper rest. Blankets were packed for summer use.

The list of gear was a long one. Any of the minor items, if forgotten, could invoke a crisis. Each man was provided with two pocket knives, a compass, match box, pocket lighter, flashlight and twelve batteries, thermos bottle, belt axe and sheath, large belt knife, rifle and rifle case.

Prices indicated the times. A rifle cost $35, sleeping bag $45, compass $5, flashlight $2, and batteries 25¢. Skis were $2 a pair, and snowshoes $12 a pair.

The herders took along skis which they would don for trailing deer over the snow. The slats were longer and wider than those used today — more like "boards" worn in ski-jumping contests. Pine tar was one of the concoctions utilized in providing a running surface for them. Other mixtures used were beeswax and paraffin.

Snowshoes were needed as well. Around camp, a man would not bother to strap on skis to do his chores. Snowshoes were simpler and easier to manipulate among the sleds, ropes, and piles of supplies. They were also valuable in breaking trail for sleds in deep snow.

Forty deer sleds, 60 harnesses, and 100 halters were stocked for the journey. Assorted lariats for staking sled deer, and for pull lines and repairs, were a necessity.

Five tents were packed, including one special double-walled rig for extremely cold weather. Six rectangular "Yukon" stoves were included to heat the tents, complemented by six alcohol-burning primus units. The latter were to be used in treeless areas.

Cooking kits, ammunition, lanterns, axes, cow bells, watches, and miner's candles were part of the vast array of incidentals not to be left behind. The list seemed endless; never before had an expedition of this nature taken place. Assembling, partitioning, and packing these items for ease of distribution could only be accomplished by men such as Bahr who had spent a lifetime so engaged. Yet even he had never attempted a drive for so long a period as was projected for this one.

The budget reflected the magnitude of the venture. The Lomen estimate for food per man was $1,095 or $13,140 a year for 12 men. Personal gear was estimated at $12,000 for the drive. The total cost, including salaries for two years, was budgeted at $97,000. This included the purchase of five sheep dogs from ranching magnate Andrew Little of Boise, Idaho, and incorporation of three dogs trained with deer in Alaska.

The herd that was finally assembled totalled 3,442 semi-wild young reindeer, most of which were one- and two-year-olds. They were more apt to survive the rugged conditions of the drive, and were also less likely to bolt for the home range than older animals. The deer were apportioned as follows: 2,890 females, 305 males, and 247 steers, roughly scaled at ten females for each bull. The steers would be used as sled deer.

PART TWO

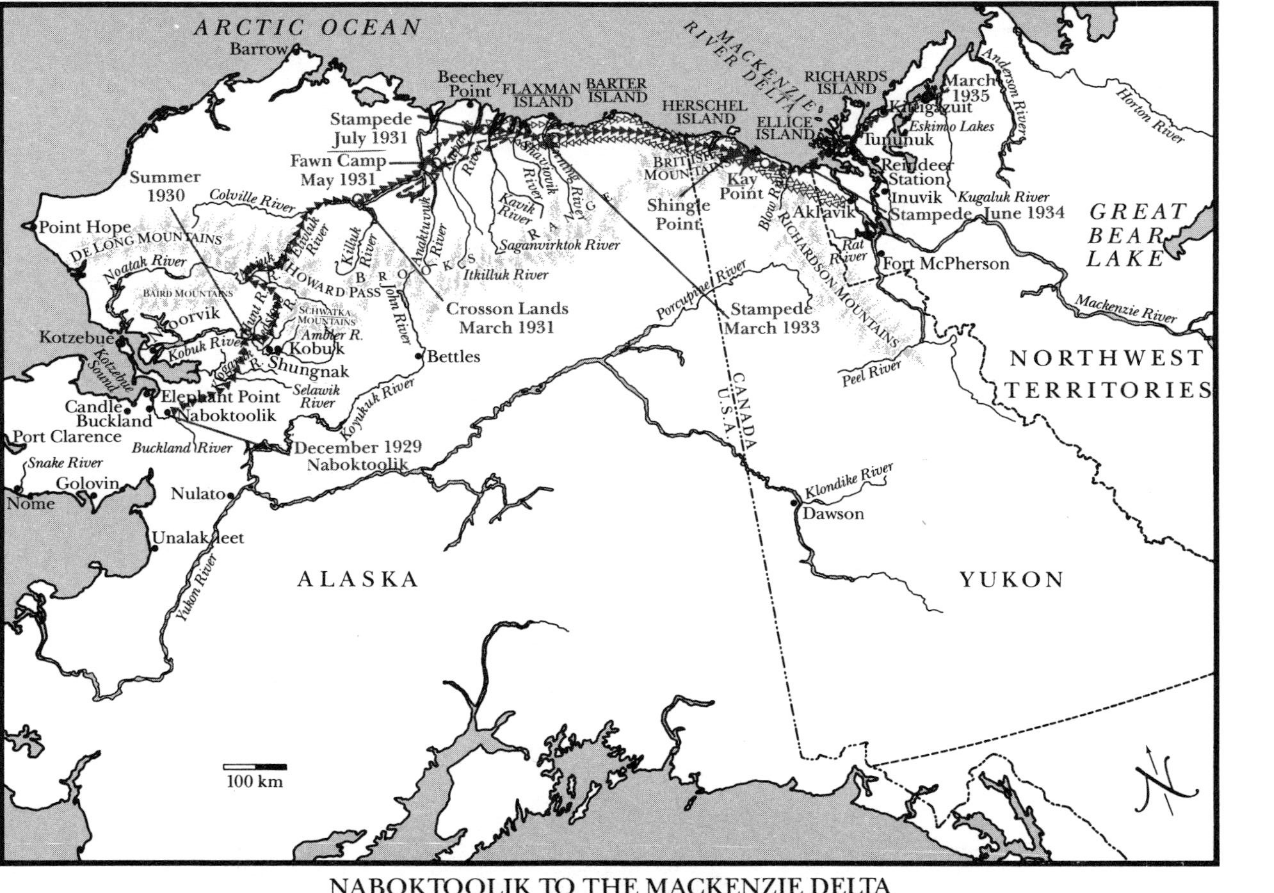

NABOKTOOLIK TO THE MACKENZIE DELTA

The First Year

CHAPTER 4

Off on the Wrong Foot

It is doubtful that any trail drive of such magnitude was ever launched with less fanfare. There were no celebrities, no speeches, no crowds, nor six-guns going off into the air, nor even relatives of the drovers on hand to wish them godspeed. In fact, it looked like the drive might not start out at all because of the lack of sled deer to haul supplies. Bahr had over-estimated the number of sledders around Naboktoolik; needing at least sixteen, he found but three, which meant he would have to quickly train thirteen more. The assembled herd had already consumed most of the forage around the camp so he culled thirteen steers to be trained, and sent the herd on its way under the tutelage of veterans Mike Nilluka and Ivar West. They set out on December 26, 1929. The temperature was thirty below zero Fahrenheit, moderate in a country where the mercury often hit fifty below, and occasionally seventy below zero.

The herd of deer formed a half-mile-long undulating mass. From the air it might have appeared as a giant, formless amoeba, slowly moving across the land, constantly changing shape as it moved. The animals stood out against a sallow glow created by the sun which sulked below the rim of the globe for most of the day.

The perpetual twilight disclosed the herd as a montage of dark heads, grayish-white necks and shoulders, brown flanks, white rumps, dusky legs, and ponderous antlers that seemed almost top-heavy on some of the deer. The average reindeer was six to seven feet in length from the nose to the end of its stubby tail, and weighed three hundred pounds.

The fact that only two men could move such a large herd, at least for a short distance, was due to the psychological make-up of the animals. Like sheep they would follow if another went first.

A steady wind coursing in from the south was the principal complicating factor as the deer were herded out across the tundra. Since reindeer prefer to walk into the wind rather than with it, they hankered to quarter off on a tangent. The reason for this predisposition is that deer like to be able to scent what is ahead of them. (And in summer, walking against the wind keeps flies and mosquitoes at bay. Conversely, when travelling with the wind, the insects leisurely glide along with it, and with the deer.) Nevertheless, the two Lapps and their herd dogs successfully managed to reach the initial objective, the low hills of the February Mountains, with a minimum of trouble.

Bahr was not completely at fault for the lack of sled deer. He had retired four years earlier and was unaware that deer were being used less and less as draft animals in populated areas, due to their vulnerability. Dogs running loose, and even in harness, would occasionally attack sled deer. Bahr had fallen victim to such a sortie a decade before he retired. He was run over by a dog team bent on the slaughter of his sledders. Lying on his back, he knifed several of the brutes in the stomach and drove them off, but not before one of his precious reindeer was flung down and killed.

The Lomens had taken this possibility into account and had laid out a route to avoid all settlements. This consideration had led Bahr to risk using deer rather than sled dogs to tote supplies because, for one thing, dog food had to be packed along to feed the canines, while deer could live off the land. Another advantage of deer was that they could haul and pack more weight than a dog. For example, at a reindeer fair held in 1917 in Alaska, one deer quite easily hauled up to a ton for a limited distance, while an entire dog team was needed for an equivalent result. Deer were also faster than dogs. *One* deer could pull a sled and driver over a ten-mile course in forty minutes while an average five-dog team took up to an hour.

Counterbalancing the reindeer's greater strength was the fact that sled deer garnered little rest when turned loose to graze, and thus tended to tire out after a few days. Dogs, if well-fed each day, did not have to hunt for food and so recovered their strength more quickly on a daily basis.

Bahr and the rest of the crew undertook the task of training the sled deer. Though this looked to be relatively simple, it took years of experience to be able to carry it off quickly and efficiently.

A two-piece wooden collar, fastened by thongs, was placed around the steer's neck, and along with it a band was run around its body just back of the forelegs. Side straps from the collar were attached to the body band. The deer was allowed to get used to this paraphernalia for a short time. Next, it was hooked to a sled with an extra long rope that extended from the underside of the band back between its hind legs. Upon being hooked up, the reindeer was given its head to run free, pulling the sled and driver across the tundra. A novice sled deer will instinctively veer toward another deer if it sees one, so a veteran sledder was pegged along the route of the beginner. When the trainee saw the other deer and stopped next to it, it was placed in harness with the older animal. The team was driven this way for a few miles, and by the end of this time the "apprentice" was supposed to know what to do.

Bahr completed the training in a few days, but in doing so sacrificed efficiency for speed. The range examiner, W. B. Miller, who was accompanying the herd for the first stages, gave his own view of the extremely truncated training, based on many years engaged in studying the animals:

"A good, well-broken sled deer is one which has been used for two years." He went on, "The first year he should be broken with great care and in the gentlest manner possible until he is trained to pull good-sized loads, but to do the work easily without jerking and jumping around." Miller noted that after two years of such training, sled deer could be driven in strings of up to forty or fifty by only two or three men.

Bahr's deer were not trained with the same degree of patience and Miller noted the difference: "In marked contrast to this is the string of sled deer which has just been caught, tied up, and then started at heavy work after a few days time."[1]

The trail boss of this momentous field drive was starting out with a serious handicap. Deer schooled too quickly were like any other nervous draft animal: they tended to be skittish, and consequently were prone to injury. A deer seriously hurt would have to be destroyed. Aside from the financial loss, the crew would lose further time and expense to train a replacement.

Two days before the new year, Bahr put on his skis, adjusted the crude strap bindings, and set out with the sledders in the wake of the herd. The old Lapp was back among his friends, both the men and the deer they herded, out under the open sky. The pungent odour of the deer; their peculiar lowing, *ogh, ogh, ogh*; the crack of their tendons as they walked; the grace and gentleness of the animals; and, yes, even their bovine-like stubbornness, brought back fond memories of his years spent looking after them, and he realized why he had elected to go one more time to the labour he had pursued since boyhood.

In addition to his financial needs, there were additional reasons for Bahr to leave the city of Seattle, as picturesque as it was. He mused over them as he led the sled deer across the tundra: the nip of thirty-below-zero temperature against his cheeks, the crisp crunch of snow under his skis, the excited bark of the shepherd dogs as they bounded to their task, the incredible brilliance of the aurora, the expanse of the land endless as time itself, and the renewal of old friendships — swapping yarns about comrades and events and adventures long past — had brought him back though he had no illusions as to the dimensions of the job ahead of him.

Fortunately, the novice sled deer proved to be surprisingly manageable, considering their limited training, possibly because they were still on familiar ground. Bahr and his crew went ten miles the first day and camped on a ridge abundant in lichens. Bivouac was on the tundra, and in this particular area there was no wood, or even brush to burn. The men crammed into one tent, setting aside the regular wood stove in favour of a primus that burned alcohol. The mercury plunged to forty-five below zero, beyond the range at which a small camp stove could heat the large tent. And though the primus was sufficient for warming up food and water, it did not throw off enough heat to dry out clothes soaked in sweat from a day's work. The cold created an eerie atmosphere in the shelter. "So dense was the fog," wrote Miller in his journal, "from our breath and the warmth of our bodies that one could not see lighted candles across the tent."

The next morning, half frozen from the uncomfortable night, their clothes still damp and clammy, the men hitched up the sled deer and set out. Late in the afternoon they caught up with Nilluka, West, and the main herd, finally bringing together all of the components of the drive for the first time. That evening the entire crew bedded down in a ravine where there was alder brush for fuel, making it possible to fire up the wood stove. As a result, the sled deer contingent spent a much more comfortable night than the previous one.

The first few nights of the drive everyone crowded into one tent. Later, three or four tents were put up, depending on the temperature and the availability of fuel. When the drovers elected to remain in an area for several weeks or months, extra canvas shelters for mess and supply were utilized.

A ritual was followed when camp was made. First, the snow was trampled down by men on showshoes or skis. Next, the tent was put up and the sleeping area covered with reindeer or caribou skins. The rectangular Yukon stove was placed on green willows or driftwood (from creeks) and the stove pipe run up through a pipe guard that protected the canvas of the tent. A fire was started immediately. Since heat rises, the warmest part of the tent was the crown. The men rigged a rope from the cross bracing and hung from it all of the clothes that needed to be dried while the men slept. Candles provided light. Before turning in, the drovers enjoyed a smoke, repaired equipment, or read magazines that were toted along, or if they could not read, scanned the white man's "looking papers" as the periodicals were called by the Eskimos. And, of course, the men talked, swapping stories about the day's events as well as those of yesteryear.

A routine was quickly established. Each morning the men on duty with the herd scrambled out of their reindeer-skin sleeping bags, and went through the monotonous procedure of putting on their gear. This included two sets of deer skins, the "underwear" with the hair turned in against the body, and the outer clothes comprised of a reindeer-skin parka and hood lined with a wolverine-fur ruff, and reindeer-skin pants, both with the hair turned out. The clothing was worn loosely to allow for movement, and also so heat would be trapped between the folds. Mittens, like the clothes, were of double thickness. Often they were attached by a lanyard to the parkas to safeguard against loss. The function of a hood was to trap heat around the head and to keep snow off one's neck. Usually a tok (wool hat) was worn underneath the hood.

Knee-length reindeer- or caribou-skin boots called mukluks were slipped on over wool socks and sealskin soles. Since they allowed for air circulation and evaporation of moisture, one's feet remained dry and warm in the coldest weather.

The Lapps' traditional dress was different than the Eskimos', but the Norsemen deferred to the traditional native garments because they were more easily obtained. Occasionally, however, the Lapps wore their four-cornered, handwoven, red and yellow wool hats, and their traditional boots which were turned up at the ends, and in which they stuffed dry grass for insulation. The calves of their legs were bound with red puttees when they used this style of boot.

The presence of alder at the ravine camp provided sufficient fuel, but it also added an obstacle in the way of an almost impenetrable thicket. The deer balked at walking through the dense scrub, and it fell to Nilluka, whom Bahr had selected as the main scout of the expedition, to find a path through the bush. While Nilluka was engaged in his search, two sled deer ran away from camp, and proved almost impossible to catch. Every time a herdsman approached and hurled a lasso at the deserters, the deer would jump nimbly aside and trot off. The delay caused by the evasive deer meant Bahr and his men saw out the year in the same camp.

Little did Andy Bahr realize on New Year's Eve, 1929, that he would still be on the trail five years hence, and that a world which had been relatively tranquil when he first started out would have seen fortunes crumble, bread lines become common, and totalitarian states arise as an almost inevitable consequence of a depression which, plague-like, circled the earth. In 1929, Herbert Hoover was president of the United States. His counterpart in Canada was Prime Minister Mackenzie King. The German *Graf Zeppelin* circled the planet that year, the first lighter-than-air craft to do so. Connie Mack's Athletics brought the world baseball championship to Philadelphia for the first time in a decade and a half, and a Canadian, Percy Williams, reigned as the one-hundred-meter and two-hundred-meter Olympic dash champion. Prohibition was still in force in the United States. At the opposite end of the world from Bahr and the reindeer drive, Admiral Richard E. Byrd completed the first successful airplane flight over the South Pole that same year.

New Year's day the two fractious sled deer were caught, but the fact that they had fled in the first place and cost the drive two days in lost time fulfilled Miller's prophecy that the semi-wild deer would cause trouble.

Bahr and his entourage plodded forward. The drive now took on its pattern of individual responsibilities. Nilluka ventured as much as five miles ahead on skis, operating as a scout. His job was to avoid alder and willow thickets that could deter the reindeer, and to make sure there was sufficient forage ahead of the herd. He did this by periodically scraping back the snow to gauge the growth of lichens, the primary winter food of the deer. He was expected to pick out a campsite at the end of each day as well.

Bahr initially glided on skis in front of the animals as a point man. Coming more slowly behind, he followed Nilluka's tracks while his men watched after the flanks and rear of the herd. West and Kingeak, along with Shelby David, August Ome, and Tom Nakkala patrolled the perimeter of the flock. Sam Segeok, Andrew Bango, and David Henry escorted the sixteen sled deer that hauled supplies and camp gear. The chores were interchangeable, depending upon the shift to which each man was assigned.

Through those first three weeks, Bahr and his men were able to gain only forty-seven miles, or an average of a little over two miles a day. Just about every conceivable situation arose during this period to slow down the drive, and at the same time to bring out the cantankerous traits of the deer.

The route lay across the valleys of a number of creeks that drained into Selawik Lake. These watercourses were overgrown with dense brush through which it was difficult to drive the fussy reindeer.

A male wolf's tracks were spotted and though the drovers did not see him, the lobo's attention to the herd was intense. His trail showed clearly that he was circling the reindeer, intent on making a kill.

The deer, too, knew the wolf was there, and became more nervous the longer he lingered on the periphery of the herd. They came to another creek with a particularly dense alder and willow thicket, and the reindeer balked at walking into it. The heavy cover was perfect camouflage for the predator and the deer's instincts warned them away. Bahr, already impatient from the frequent delays, pushed the sensitive animals too hard, crowding dogs and men up on the heels of the ungulates in a grand effort to push them forward. That was a mistake: about 200 deer split off and bolted for the home range. The trail boss debated whether or not to go after the malcontents, and then decided in favour of the move. Realizing that the dollar value of the deer was worth the effort, he told his men they would have to reverse the direction of the *entire* herd in order to pick up the deserters. It would be impossible to lead the mavericks back alone; the only way to reincorporate them into the main herd would be to bring the larger group in close proximity of the smaller one, whereupon the smaller group would instinctively merge with the larger. Individualists the deer were not.

Using the range dogs to advantage, the drovers turned the main herd around and down the back trail. Within a day the vagabonds were reabsorbed into the larger group. The wolf disappeared, possibly scared off by the ringing of cow bells attached at random to twenty of the deer.

No sooner was the roundup of the deer

completed than a storm struck the drive like a battering ram. Whenever the ice pack retreated, leaving open water, the air warmed up and absorbed evaporated moisture. Prevailing westerlies picked up the moisture which precipitated as snow when the winds collided with cooler air over the land. The herdsmen were forced to make camp on the crest of an exposed ridge, where they quickly put up their tent by draping it over a frame made of two sleds. The storm lashed the fragile shelter for two days before it finally moderated, leaving two feet of wet snow.

The tempest further illustrated the fickle nature of the deer. The presence of food beneath the snow often dictated whether a herd remained where it was or fled when hit by severe weather. In this case, the deer were grazing in an area heavy with lichen and the mass of animals stayed put. The exigency of food had won out over the urge to run.

The labours of Hercules had nothing on the travails of Bahr and his men. A sharp rise in temperature followed the blizzard, converting the snow into a glue-like slop in which the supply sleds slid and tilted at angles more akin to a sinking ship than a sled. This made the going extremely toilsome for the men who had to bodily assist the draft deer pulling the sleds.

Every stream bed or hilly ridge presented another problem: reindeer's wariness of going downhill. The herd balked again as they approached a hill overlooking Kouchak Lakes. The reluctance of the deer to descend the slope took on the characteristics of a battle of wills as the drovers strove to uproot the reindeer. The intractable ungulates were equally as adamant in refusing to budge. Every time the men pushed too hard, the deer would go into a mill. This was the last thing the herdsmen wanted to see, and it was happening all too often. The mill was a defensive mechanism. When the deer felt threatened, the herd circled in on itself with the weaker animals and fawns quickly working their way to the centre of the herd. The stronger animals moved to the outer perimeter for the purpose of fending off attacks. The mill began to accelerate, at first slowly, then faster and faster, until the entire coterie whirled in unison, like a spinning top, with the deer on the periphery racing at top speed. The only way the herders could stop the revolving mass was to slacken the pressure by backing off fifty or a hundred yards. Once the deer perceived there was no danger, the merry-go-round slowed to a halt and the animals resumed grazing.

The worst thing about the mill was that it occasionally gained so much speed that, as if subject to centrifugal force, it flew apart, ending up in a stampede, or series of small breakaways. When this happened, the deer became vulnerable to predators and the subsequent roundup was a great drain on the herders.

The stalemate at Kouchak lasted for several days. It was finally broken when several sledders were led back and forth a number of times through the worst places in order to break a trail through the dense underbrush, and the others were coaxed into following along.

The warm spell hung on. A heavy rain suddenly swept in making the soft snow even worse. It became next to impossible for the sled deer to proceed without a trail being broken for them. Bahr elected to use the main herd to break trail for the sledders rather than the other way around. Yet, because *driving* the herd often instigated the mill, the drovers became irritated by Bahr's strategy. They felt the sled deer should be put to the fore in order to *entice* the herd to follow in the more typical manner, and in that way prevent milling.

Circling was to occur again and again, yet Bahr persisted in his refusal to use the sled deer as trail breakers. He maintained that the first leg of the trip was a learning experience for the herd as much as for the men. Miller quoted Bahr:

"We are now just training," the trail boss said. "Training sled deer, training the herd, training dogs, and training men. I must do much talking now to tell and show how things must be done. Bye and Bye everyone will know what to do."

Mother Nature gave no quarter. A sudden drop in temperature froze the rain-drenched land, blanketing the tundra with a coat of ice. The reindeer attempted to paw their way through the solid surface to get at the lichens underneath, but it was a futile effort as the ice was too thick. The only alternative for Bahr was to keep pressing the herd forward until the deer either found ice-free patches or other forms of vegetation on which they could feed. And, as if that was not bad enough, a snow squall followed the downpour. The wind that pushed the snow was so fierce a man could almost lean against it. Several deer broke away from the herd. It looked like a mill was going to form again, so Bahr slacked off the pressure and again ordered the men to lead several sled deer ahead of the herd. This act successfully enticed the rest of the animals to follow along behind the sledders and a stampede was avoided.

Yet, as Bahr had feared, moving the sled deer to the front of the drive under such conditions took its toll. Some of the draft animals were injured or worn out by the strain of pulling a sled through heavy snow, and required prompt replacement.

The sled deer were not alone in their agony. W. B. Miller by this time was suffering acutely from the cold and exertion. Miller was in as good condition as the average man accustomed to the outdoors, but was not strong enough to withstand the blizzards, alternating rain and heavy snow, gyrating temperatures, and the constant grinding psychological and physical distress of trying to keep up with men to whom the struggle was second nature, and who were accustomed to surviving in the most savage climate on earth.

Yet another casualty was Mike Nilluka, who was troubled by a stomach disorder, probably brought on by the cold or the crude conditions under which the drovers sometimes gulped down half-cooked food.

Having been almost a month on the trail, Bahr saw this as a fitting time to make camp for a few days. Nilluka was suffering so much from his belly ailment that Bahr sent him back to the coast to see a doctor when a dog team became available. Miller, on the other hand, decided to stick it out a little longer. Bahr decided this was a good time to train more sled deer, so his men rounded up eight likely looking animals and proceeded to work them into harness. It took two days before Bahr was satisfied. He again put the herd on the move, veering from an easterly to a northerly direction, and crossed to the north bank of the Selawik river. A trapper offered Miller a ride at this point, and he, too, left the trail drive.

The loss of Nilluka and Miller was a setback for Bahr. Even though Miller was more of an observer than an active participant, his assistance would be missed. Nilluka's loss was more important; he was a veteran who knew reindeer and their habits. His absence put that much more of a burden on the men who remained.

Miller proceeded to Selawik and then to Elephant Point. There he advised Crowley of the adverse conditions that had been experienced by Bahr and his men. He went on to Nome where he told Alfred Lomen the same thing. Miller's comments were backed up by copious notes he had taken during the period he was with the trail drive. These trepidations centred on the slow progress of the herd, which was averaging no better than two miles a day. In reviewing the three weeks he had been with the herd, Miller cited the weather as being the principal cause for the slow progress. One entire week out of the three, the herd was raked by blizzards, prohibiting any travel at all. The antics of the animals, ranging from frequent stampedes to desertions of sled deer, cost the drive three days. Thus, out of three weeks, the herd only moved forward on eleven days. These statistics were enough to incite Lomen to write to Dan Crowley suggesting he visit the herd to ascertain what assistance could be rendered Bahr, if any.

While Miller was making his report, Bahr's troubles seemed to go on and on. The up and down variations of the temperatures over the next several weeks were confusing. Frequently, a thaw would be followed by a plunge of the mercury, creating a crust on the snow not quite thick enough to hold the drovers' weight. As a result, they broke through at every step, making it extremely tiring to proceed.

When they reached the Kuchuk River Bahr called for another rest period, and proceeded to break in more sled deer. By now, the drive had been on the trail for thirty-four days, and had gone barely fifty miles. This meant their average had deteriorated to little better than a mile a day. At this rate, they would be fortunate to reach the Hunt River cache before fawning time in April.

Dan Crowley, after hearing from Lomen, quickly rounded up a pilot and, on the last day of January, flew from Elephant Point to Kotzebue. He sought out Nilluka, who had travelled on to Kotzebue from Elephant Point in order to be treated there by the resident doctor. The Lapp was up and around by this time, but was too weak to go back to the herd.

The flight was delayed several days in Kotzebue due to the usual topsy-turvy weather of the region. Finally, Crowley and pilot Victor Ross, along with a guide, Jack Hooper, took off for the reindeer camp.

The biplane was of the open cockpit type, which at the prevailing temperature of thirty below zero, was close to the lower limit the plane could fly. Ross did not know the location of the reindeer herd, but because his two passengers, at least, had a general idea of where it was, they were given the unenviable task of peering outside the cockpit to give the pilot directions. After only ninety seconds of exposure to the bitter cold, both men suffered frostbitten cheeks.

Ross flew southeast from Kotzebue to cross diagonally over Hotham Inlet and the Kobuk delta. Peering to his left, Crowley could see Noorvik, a tree-blessed hamlet on a channel of the Kobuk River. As the flight progressed over the gleaming white world of the delta, they overflew Selawik Lake and the town of the same name. They dropped a mail sack on the town, and from the size of the crowd, Crowley judged the plane was one of the few that had ever flown over the village.

The men flew on and enjoyed an eagle-eye's view of the Kotzebue basin. Finally, Ross brought the plane into a landing at the camp of Hooper's brother forty miles up the Selawik River, breaking a ski strut in the process. Ross set to work to repair the damage, which required staying all night. Dan learned from Hooper's brother that the herd was only ten miles distant. Since there was no dog team available, he decided to snowshoe in. The next day, after a valiant struggle, the superintendent reached Bahr's camp, where he found the trail boss hard at work training sled deer.

Bahr was pleasantly surprised to see Crowley, and took the opportunity to inform him that his goal would be to reach the Kobuk by spring, rather than to go farther on as had been the original plan.[2] He explained that the herd was in poor condition because of milling and stampeding. The marches and countermarches had worn out the deer. Bahr estimated they had walked two hundred miles for every fifty they travelled in a straight line.

The Laplander told Crowley he thought it would be better to spend the spring and summer on the Kobuk, where supplies could easily be obtained by boat from Kotzebue, than to push the herd into the mountains where the problem of resupply would be much more difficult. Also, incursions of indigenous caribou would be a constant threat, as the deer were prone to drift off with their wild cousins if a herd larger than theirs passed through the area.

Dan Crowley perceived the drovers to be in good

humour, but whether this observation was correct in view of his short stay at the camp, was doubtful. This seemed doubly so since Bahr himself was to state only three weeks later that some of his men wanted to quit.

During February the vagaries of the weather, and intolerable obstacles persisted. No sooner had the drive set out again after Crowley departed than it ran into an impasse in the form of a forest of willows and alders so dense the men actually found it necessary to hack their way through the thickets with their belt axes. This was no easy task because of the rubbery resilience of the scrub trees. In this growth, the snow had little chance to pack down and harden. It was so deep the sleds were constantly bogging down, putting everyone into a bad humour.

The deer, too, were becoming more cantankerous. The herd was passing through an area that had been swept the previous summer by a tundra fire that destroyed the lichen. Now the deer were scraping back the snow and finding no food. There was no way of telling how extensive the damage was, so Bahr pushed the deer forward as quickly as possible. Luckily, the reindeer walked out of the burn area before they became overly weak.

By now, the drive was nearing a tributary of the Kobuk and the first leg of the arduous journey was almost over; but the recriminations were not. The Eskimos were disgruntled for two reasons: one, because they were paid considerably less than the lowest-paid Lapp, though most of them had as much or more experience; and two, some of them were not satisfied with Bahr's leadership. Even some of the Lapps were irritated with Bahr. They felt that his intransigence in not using sled deer more often to lead the herd was the reason for the constant milling and resultant irritatingly slow progress of the trail drive.

Crowley, too, was not altogether happy with Bahr's leadership abilities. He was convinced that Bahr had made a mistake in not moving to Naboktoolik earlier in the fall to round up the deer and to train sledders. Crowley viewed Bahr's procrastination as the cause of the drive's delay.

On balance, Crowley understood that there were many aspects of the expedition over which the Lapp had no control, and for which he could not be blamed. Dan knew Bahr had not set the wages which were the root cause of the Inuit's disaffection, and also that Bahr could not manipulate the weather. As bad as the climate was in the Kotzebue basin, it was not always *that* bad. Nor was Andrew at fault for the wild condition of the deer which had been afield all summer. Though the total distance travelled was meagre, the entire herd was still en route, which is what really mattered that first winter.

CHAPTER 5

Reindeer Station

While Bahr struggled through that first winter to push the giant herd to the prearranged supply point on the banks of the Kobuk River, the Canadian Department of the Interior went ahead with plans to set up a camp to receive the reindeer in the delta of the Mackenzie River.

Oswald Finnie, Director of the Northwest Territories and Yukon branch of the department, sent for Bob Porsild as soon as the latter returned from a vacation in Denmark. Finnie assigned to him the task of choosing the site for the station, as well as building the camp. On March 14, 1930, Porsild set out for Aklavik in company with Wilhelm Hatting, a former trader from Bob's hometown in Greenland whom he had hired as an assistant. The two were destined to run into an adventure even before they reached Aklavik. They boarded a plane and flew successfully from Edmonton to the first stop at Fort Resolution. After helping the pilot unload supplies there, Hatting and Porsild climbed back aboard the plane and took off again. The aircraft was airborne only a few minutes when the engine failed and they crashed. The three men crawled out of the wreckage unhurt, but it was a near fatal experience for all of them as the plane was a total loss. Bob then walked fifteen miles without snowshoes to summon a rescue party that fetched his companions back to Fort Resolution.

Another plane was called in and eight days later Porsild and Hatting were airborne again. This time they reached Aklavik successfully, landing in front of the tiny community on the west channel of the Mackenzie River on the twenty-second of March.

The general plan for building the reindeer station was perfected and drawn up by Bob's brother. He had submitted the concept to Finnie, who approved it. Under older methods of construction that were once in place in Alaska, reindeer were simply driven into enclosures made out of split poles buried in the ground, looking almost like scaled-down versions of an old western stockade. These permanent fixtures afforded no portability. After one or two roundups, the pasture in which the deer grazed could be destroyed for years to come.

Recalling a solution favoured by the Lomen brothers, Erling Porsild suggested that prefabricated, movable corrals be used. These were made of rough lumber in twelve-by-seven-foot sections that were leaned up against wooden posts implanted in the ground along the corral at twelve-foot intervals. Herders could erect the enclosure in a matter of a few hours; when ready to move on, the sections could easily be disassembled and transported to another grazing area, leaving only the supporting posts behind. In this case, using the newer style of enclosure spared Bob the unenviable job of cutting about one hundred cords of poles that would have been required under the old system. He would still need, of course, to cut up enough logs to shore up the sections, and to build the main house and herders' cabins.

Bob Porsild's first duty was to find logs for the project. He and Hatting set out on April 12 with two dog teams and mushers James Edwards and Joe Greenland, whom he had hired to transport them to a timber patch sixty miles east of Aklavik. Another man, Jack Bowen, was engaged to pick up Bob and his partner on May 10. After two days on the trail, they found the right spot. The mushers dropped them off and returned home. The task of the two men would have been easier if they had kept one of the dog teams, as sled dogs were commonly used for hauling logs to build cabins and to stock up on firewood.

The tree line ran east and west across the Mackenzie delta from Aklavik. The growth here was composed of spruce trees that were spindly when compared to similar species that grow in more temperate climates. The logging job took Porsild and Hatting almost the full month Bob had allotted for the task. They cut timbers ten feet in length for corral posts, logs of assorted sizes ranging from ten to fourteen feet for cabins, and longer, twenty-four-foot beams for buildings. It was gruelling labour harvesting timber in the deep snow. The fallers had to be extra careful that the trees toppled in the proper direction. If wrong in their judgement, they risked serious injury because their mobility was severely handicapped by the snowshoes they wore.

The chores were more formidable in a mantle of snow. When a tree fell, the men had to dig it out in order to trim it, and then, like draft horses, harness up and skid the logs out to the river bank.

The vicious elements added drama to each day a man was abroad in the Arctic. After completing the job of cutting logs, the two men wondered why Bowen had not shown up. They were in a vulnerable position, across the river from Aklavik on the east side of the delta.

Porsild wrote: "Jack Bowen did not arrive till in the evening the 16th of May, delayed by flooded ice around Aklavik. We were mainly living on fried rats [muskrats] for the last week in camp. Ice not thick this winter so had a rather hard time getting back, breaking through both men and dogs several times. Back evening the 18th of May."

The combination of hard work and lack of food had its effect on Porsild. "I lost 24 pounds in weight during the 4 weeks woodcutting, which is rather hard work at this time of the year and without a dog team."[1]

Coinciding with Porsild's labours on the east channel of the Mackenzie River was the processing of lumber orders, which Finnie forwarded at Bob's request. It was of crucial importance to the reindeer project that the lumber be shipped that summer. Planks were not available in the delta. Upriver, Finnie, in the interest of fairness, decided to award half of the order for ten thousand board feet to one company, and half to another. As is often the case with an executive who has had considerable experience in dealing with supplies, Finnie's sixth sense envisioned a foul-up. This spurred him to stress to his employees working along the length of the Mackenzie to scrupulously examine and count the planks before they were accepted.

The contracts were awarded to two small mills, the lumber received, and the vouchers signed. The planks were then shipped downriver to Aklavik.

Bob Porsild, in the meantime, sought out three men to work for him for the summer of 1930. The principal problem in trying to hire anyone was the overlap of the proposed summer work with the springtime muskrat trapping season. Frank Carmichael, a local trapper, and Hans Hansen, another trapper and personal friend of Bob's, agreed to work for him, but held out for the amount of funds (about seventy-five dollars) they would lose from missing the remainder of the muskrat season which ran through the first week of June, *plus* the full month's salary. Bob wanted each man to work for three full months (June to August), at one hundred dollars a month. The young Dane solved this difficulty with Solomon-like judgement. He evened out the pay and suggested a rate of one hundred and twenty-five dollars a month instead, but no bonus for lost trapping time. They agreed. Porsild also hired John McDonald, from Fort McPherson, at seventy-five dollars a month.

The question now was where to build the reindeer station? Bob and Erling had previously espied from the air the abandoned Eskimo community of Kittigazuit, situated at the mouth of the Mackenzie River's east channel. They thought it might make a good place for the reindeer station, so as soon as the ice went out Bob went downriver by boat to check it out. However, on approaching the settlement, he became disenchanted with a maze of low islands and mud flats screening Kittigazuit, and elected instead to set up the station at a bend in the river to the south. He wrote: "We finally decided to choose a place about seven miles above [south of] Kittigazuit called by the natives Kooryuak, an old husky [that is, Eskimo] settlement along a small creek. The country behind offers several advantages for placing the corral, as far as I could estimate from hikes in the neighborhood."[2] The advantages were the seemingly unlimited pasture for the deer, easy access from the river, and open terrain conducive to herding. The lack of timber near the camp motivated a transfer about sixty miles upriver a few years later. The second, permanent camp was called simply Reindeer Station.

Porsild and his men went about moving the logs to the site and commenced building the reindeer complex. The planks for the interior work and the portable corrals were due to arrive, so Bob went to Aklavik to pick them up. When he got there, he was appalled at what he saw. The boards dispatched by the Liard Coal Company, at Fort Simpson, were thrown helter-skelter onto the shore, and were in shoddy condition. This was in stark contrast to the carefully bundled lumber from the other firm, the Wynn Company at Grand Detour, with which Finnie had placed an order.

The sizes of the planks from the Liard Coal Company were such a mismatch, that it was impossible to measure them, or verify that the correct number of board feet had been shipped, without taking what Porsild deemed was an unnecessary amount of time. He complained: "How much lumber there is I can not estimate, the lumber not being bundled and not two pieces in the whole lot of the same length and thickness. Most of it is of an average thickness of 3/4 inch, and too thin for our purpose, and it looks to me as if Mr. Cousins, the owner, considered this order a splendid chance to get rid of a lot of offal not saleable to anybody but the government."[3]

Bob estimated the lumber to be two thousand board feet short, but had no choice other than to sign the bill of lading; it was impractical to send an order back to the shipper when he was located seven hundred miles up the Mackenzie River. He advised Finnie not to pay for it; then promptly departed Aklavik for the site of the reindeer camp, about one hundred and fifty miles away, and with no avenues of communication.

Finnie refused to pay for the mismatched lumber, whereupon Cousins sued the federal government. The parties to the dispute continued to haggle while Bob Porsild, who had ignited the furor, was secure at the reindeer camp and aloof from the infighting.

Finally, after a series of one hundred and twenty-two messages had been exchanged, Dr. U. A. Urquhart, government agent at Aklavik, took the responsibility of stating that the pile received had indeed been five thousand board feet. Finnie, relieved that someone had officially owned up to the fact that the total was correct, authorized payment to the company.

Porsild's unavailability was not entirely his own fault, since a wireless service was not always accessible, even when he was in Aklavik, but it was plain that Finnie was irritated with him. The director wired his complaints from Ottawa, objecting to the way the Dane had handled the lumber order, and added a few more gripes about the operation in general and about unauthorized expenditures.

Anecdotes from this correspondence were not always grim. Bob had wired Finnie that a typewriter he was supposed to be using was not in working order, and would be returned. Finnie replied by letter wherein he patiently explained that the typewriter had been thoroughly overhauled and rebuilt in the department's machine shop in Ottawa before it was sent north. He explained that the typewriter, providing no damage had been incurred in the shipment, should have been in good condition when Porsild received it.

Bob Porsild gained the last word in this exchange when he wrote Finnie on the typewriter. Each time he came to a numeral key (none worked), he left a space and wrote in the number by hand!

By the end of the summer of 1930, Porsild could look at his accomplishments with satisfaction. Firstly, he had found a suitable place for the reindeer station. Secondly, he had hired a crew at reasonable wages; and thirdly, he put up the buildings needed. To successfully fulfill these tasks in such an isolated area was no mean accomplishment.

However, one chore had not yet been completed and it loomed over Porsild and his crew with the irksome persistence of an unpaid bill. This was the construction of the chutes and corrals.

An even more salient event was scheduled with regards to Bob Porsild's private life, this being the pending arrival of his fiancée, Elly Rothe Hansen, whom he had met many years before when he attended school in her hometown, Soro, Denmark. Her recollections have given an enlightening insight into what life was really like on the northern frontier.

Elly arrived at Aklavik by riverboat in mid-September. Since Bob was on a tight schedule, no time was lost with respect to wedding plans, and they were married in the tiny Anglican church by Reverend Murray the day after Elly disembarked. A Mountie from the local detachment, Arthur Fielding, in full dress uniform escorted her to the altar, where Bob and his best man, Hans Hansen, waited, along with bridesmaid Dorothy Cunningham, a nurse from the area. Their exchange of vows was reported to be the first all-white marriage ever held in Aklavik.

No sooner had the ceremony ended than someone shouted "Steamboat!" and Bob and the best man rushed pell-mell to the boat, leaving the bride standing almost alone at the altar — albeit *after* the marriage. The bridesmaid provided company for Elly while the groom was occupied unloading the boat. The bride wondered why the steamboat appeared to be more important to the populace than the wedding. She was advised that the boat — the last one of the season — held the government's winter allotment of liquor, which amounted to twelve bottles for each white family. Natives were not permitted to drink alcohol.

That evening the owners of Aklavik's only restaurant gave a wedding dinner which featured a caribou roast with all the trimmings, and a wedding cake with icing so hard it took the combined efforts of the bride and groom to hack through it. Thirty whites were served at the first setting, followed by an equal number of natives at the second. There was more than enough food for all.

After dinner most of the guests adjourned to an empty warehouse where three Eskimo fiddlers initiated the music and the newlyweds danced the first waltz. The groom then disappeared temporarily to act as host in distributing part of his liquor allotment.

Elly found the Eskimos to be light on their feet and wonderful dancers. She enjoyed their company and recalled the native people — Loucheux Indians were also present — as being jolly and happy.

Men of the Royal Canadian Signals Corps, who ran the newly installed wireless station at Aklavik, after midnight invited the couple to their complex for tea and ham sandwiches. Bob, by this time had completed his session as host, and he and Elly danced there until four in the morning.

Thus culminated the Danish girl's first experience with the friendly camaraderie of the people of the North. The bride, however, would quickly learn that tragedy went hand in hand with good fortune in the Arctic.

The next day Bob's job necessitated his return to the reindeer station. The couple left for the camp aboard a gas boat that had in tow a scow loaded with all of their winter supplies. Also aboard were Hans Hansen, and Donald Oliver, an Eskimo youth considered by Porsild to be of outstanding promise, and whom Bob hoped to train in the reindeer business. The journey to the reindeer site took two days. Here, Elly found to her surprise that a two-storey house awaited her. Bob dutifully carried her across the threshold, and she was then free to explore her new quarters.

She appreciated the scenery: "The view was grand, water for miles and miles and the mountains in the background. There were no trees, just some willow bushes. There were no neighbours for fifteen miles, no radio, and no telephone."[4]

Mrs. Porsild discovered they were liberally supplied with food purchased from the Hudson's Bay Company. Such items as canned butter and bacon, eggs preserved in salt, condensed milk, boxes of baker's chocolate, onions, potatoes, sugar, and flour filled the larder.

One of Elly's most disagreeable chores was toting water up the steep bank from the river. This rugged task sometimes took hours, and was accomplished by using a wooden shoulder yoke for the pails. She then dumped the water into a barrel next to the stove. After freeze-up, she obtained water by filling a barrel inside the house with snow and ice which gradually melted. No matter how hard she worked, she reminisced, there never seemed to be enough water to fill the demands.

Elly and Bob often hunted ptarmigan. Bob would range ahead shooting birds, which Elly picked up and placed in a sack. Of this labour, she said: "My steps got slower and slower; the load got heavier and heavier; I didn't even get any offer to carry them home for me. Why do women always carry the heaviest burden, I only ask."[5]

Elly Porsild was in the Arctic less than four weeks

when she found out how dangerous the polar region could be. In mid-October, she and Bob along with Hansen and Oliver and the dog team motored downriver by boat to Kittigazuit, where they put the craft into dry-dock for the winter. Bob stayed behind to winterize the boat while the other three returned to the reindeer camp. Hans was to return for Bob the next day.

Oliver set out in front of the team acting as trail breaker and guide. Hans was behind the sled as musher for the dogs, and Elly rode as passenger. After travelling several miles Hansen and Oliver took a short cut across a patch of newly formed ice. The frozen surface groaned and creaked as the sled sped over it, but the commitment had been made and they kept going. Suddenly, though, the ice broke under Oliver and he disappeared in the black depths of the river.

The rent opened by Oliver's weight spread through the ice for the full length of the team. The dogs, handicapped by the harness, snapped futilely at the ice cakes as they fought to escape. In seconds, they too were gone. Elly and Hans were free of any ties to the sled and floated high because of their reindeer parkas, the hollow hairs of which made them temporarily buoyant. They were able to escape the frigid water by pulling themselves onto solid ice and crawling away from the deadly maw of the river. Thoroughly soaked and shocked by the sudden loss of Donald, they staggered back to Kittigazuit, where Bob built a fire to warm them up and dry out their clothes. This, then, was Elly Porsild's literal, horrifying baptism into the dangers of the Arctic.

While Bob Porsild struggled to complete the reindeer complex, and Andrew Bahr guided the herd of 3,500 deer to the Kobuk River, the Lomen brothers were having a difficult time keeping their reindeer operation solvent.

Meat prices had begun to slide within a few months of the stock market crash in October of 1929. As the depression widened, the Lomens were forced to sell reindeer meat in the Lower 48 for as little as twelve cents a pound. Ranchers in the United States were so desperate to unload their stock they were selling carloads of cattle and sheep for less money than it cost them to ship the animals to market in the first place!

One of the worst blows struck against the Lomen operation came from the United States government itself. The federal Department of Interior circulated a pamphlet in two hundred cities advertising reindeer meat for nine cents a pound, or three cents under the Lomen price. In light of the many years and the thousands of dollars the Lomen Company had spent on popularizing the sale of reindeer meat, this was a treacherous and near fatal blow. The Lomens simply could not ship meat to the southern market at the same rates as the government-subsidized shipments.

Yet another devastating setback occurred in California when stock growers pushed legislation through the state government which forbade the sale of uninspected meat. Since reindeer was not even included in the meat inspection act, this effectively shut down the ten-year-old Lomen operation in California, and along with it, their offices in Los Angeles and San Francisco.

The scramble for markets in competition with beef interests, while also fighting the government, was not an ideal situation in which to keep a business afloat. There is little doubt that the Canadian contract, with its first and second payments, pulled the Lomens back from the brink of a financial abyss. However, the seeds of doubt had been planted as to whether the Lomens could keep the drive afloat if it ran into serious difficulty.

CHAPTER 6

Interval on the Kobuk

The Kobuk, one of the magnificent rivers of the North in the balmy days of summer, was still smothered in snow and ice when the reindeer herd led by Andy Bahr and his ornery crew descended into its valley at the end of February, 1930. This waterway is the ninth-largest river in Alaska. Flowing 347 miles, it drains 12,000 square miles of terrain, including the rugged towers of the Baird Range and the areas of its source among the declivitous spires of the Schwatkas. Farther down it sidles past the enigmatic Great Kobuk sand dunes to filter into Hotham Inlet via a large delta.

The drovers guided the herd across the Kobuk to reach the cache Bahr had placed on the Hunt River. Shortly after they arrived, Bahr's scouts found a valley eight miles above the cache where there was plenty of edible moss available, and led the deer there. This sanctuary was surrounded by high hills and was an ideal place for fawning. An out-camp was established here.

Once the main camp was set up on the Hunt, Bahr used the respite to make his way to a trading post owned by Warren and Archie Ferguson at Shungnak, fifty miles upriver from the mouth of the Hunt. Bahr posted a letter to the Lomens, informing them of the grumbling by the dissatisfied members of the crew. Since the reindeer were safely across the Kobuk and could be held quite handily, he felt that if some of the herders resigned it would not be nearly as crucial as if they were still on the trail. Now he could hire replacements if he needed them. There was little attempt to solve the root causes of the discontent.

Fierce storms along the Kobuk in March and part of April sealed the decision of the disgruntled drovers. Three Eskimos, August Ome, Shelby David, and David Henry quit and returned to their homes at Golovin on April 10. Bahr could not convince the herders to stay, even with a promise that he would attempt to negotiate an increase in their wages. Mike Nilluka, however, had returned, coming up the Hunt with a mail delivery, having recovered from his stomach ailment.

Spring emerges suddenly in the Arctic — like a ptarmigan chick bursting from an egg. The foremost harbinger of warmth in the polar regions is the tinkling sound of water dropping — whether from a rock, or plunking from a tent guy rope, a cabin eave, or from the tip of an icicle, this event rings like a bell to one who has been enmeshed in the long Arctic winter. An unseasonal chinook occasionally gives the same results, but at the right time in the right month, the veteran Arctic dweller recognizes the unmistakable instance when the cold truly unbends.

Bahr's mundane tone in a letter disguises the intensity of feeling: "The weather is getting mild now and the snow, and, ice on the snow, will be softer, that means better feeding; anyhow spring is coming."[1]

The average gestation period for reindeer is seven months and seven days, so that the first fawns generally appear around the second week of April. Since does should be placed on good pasture in an area of little potential disturbance for at least a month before the fawns are born, the Hunt River tributary proved to be an excellent refuge for them. When the sun shone, it was refracted in the valley, and caused the ice and snow to give way to patches of green earlier than in other locations. This growth consisted of flowering stalks of cotton sedge that were rich in food values needed by does to furnish milk for their fawns.

The calves dropped throughout April and into the month of May. Approximately two thousand were born, according to Bahr's estimates. Andrew wrote to the Lomens and asked them if they wanted the animals branded, at the same time advising against it. He estimated it would cost at least two thousand dollars to accomplish this task because corrals would have to be built and extra men hired. The Lomens concurred with his judgement in this case, as the route to Canada was intentionally planned to avoid any other reindeer herds in the Arctic, negating the need for such marking.

The first days of a reindeer fawn's life are the most hazardous, as predators centred their attention on the young ones. Herders had to be alert to attacks by wolves, lynx, wolverines, grizzly bears, and eagles. Under the sharp eyes of the remaining herders, the newborn came through the most dangerous period — the first hours of their lives — with a minimum of losses.

Bahr was still vexed with the nagging question of what route to take to reach the north side of the Brooks Range, and of what method to employ to transport their supplies. After Bahr made a second trip to telegraph Alfred Lomen for assistance, Dan Crowley flew from Nome with Victor Ross in his ski-equipped plane. Having preplanned the drive to cross the Baird Mountains by way of the Hunt River, Bahr and Crowley decided to make an aerial reconnaissance of that river. If the weather held on the trip, they would fly farther north across the Noatak and continue over the DeLong peaks to the headwaters of the Colville River, surveying the second leg of the journey as well.

The plane arrived none too soon. Dr. L. E. Benson, an elderly physician, had begged the Lomens the year before to be allowed to accompany the drive. He hoped he might be of some value inoculating natives in various villages they passed near, and, of course, in tending the ills that might befall the drovers. Benson also wanted to take notes on the plant life and geology of the region through which the drive was expected to go.

The Lomens were reluctant to give permission to the doctor because they realized he was not used to such arduous living as could be expected on the drive. However, he was so persistent in his appeals — and could, in an emergency, be invaluable to an injured drover — that the Lomens consented. They sent him to the Hunt River cache to await the arrival of the herd, assuming, correctly, that the first leg of the drive would be too tough for him. Indeed, merely waiting for the herd to arrive proved to be Benson's undoing.

Tent living had resulted in the doctor becoming deeply chilled, and his health had deteriorated so badly that by the time Crowley arrived he was coughing up blood. Every time he tried to recline, phlegm accumulated in his throat, choking him, and making rest impossible.

Dan had him flown to a nearby settlement for better care, and advised the sick man he would take him back to Nome in Ross's plane when the air reconnaissance was completed. The doctor would not recover from his ordeal for many years.

Heavy clouds prevailed for nine days before the skies finally cleared enough to take off one day at noon. Ross flew straight north, following the Hunt

River. He levelled off at four thousand feet, yet the highest of the Baird peaks still loomed above the aircraft by another thousand. The mountains closed in on them as they approached the headwaters of the Hunt, narrowing their flight path down to nothing more than a canyon with abrupt banks. This was definitely not what Bahr and Crowley wanted to see. No herd could be driven through such an unforgiving gulch, proving that hearsay had been dead wrong about the Hunt. The airborne reconnaissance had saved the drive from an endless delay or possible disaster. Thereupon Crowley told Ross to look for another route.

The weather ahead of them cleared as the plane growled its way over the headwall of the Hunt to the Noatak. Ross followed the swale of the Aniuk, a tributary of the larger Noatak, to go through deceptively gentle Howard Pass and emerge on the north slope of the Brooks Range. He took the plane fifteen miles down the Etivluk River, a tributary of the Colville, from which the outline of the latter could be seen in the distance. As far as Ross could figure, they were the first humans in history to view that precise area from the air. They discerned, by the formation of the Colville valley, that it flowed east at this point, rather than west as shown on some government maps. After clearing the northern foothills, the vast, flat, white Arctic prairie lay before them. This expanse of alabaster was broken only by opaque outlines of alder-and-willow-encased creeks that tumbled north to the Arctic Ocean.

The men spotted caribou along the Etivluk River. This was a good sign, as it meant there would be forage for the reindeer. Three barren-ground grizzlies, newly up and around after their winter's sleep, were seen prowling about and from the altitude of the plane over the untimbered land, looked like a trio of ground squirrels.

Finally, the limits of fuel dictated the need for turning the aircraft around. Pilot Ross steered the plane back over the abutment of the Brooks Range to search for a route across the Baird Mountains as an alternative to the precipitous upper canyon of the Hunt River. They flew down the Redstone River and found it satisfactory for driving a herd.

The men had been in the air for three and a half hours when the plane touched down on the ice in front of the camp on the Hunt, their trip an unqualified success. There was no doubt as to the route the drive would follow, at least across the Brooks Range; nor were there any reservations that a plane could successfully carry supplies across the mountain barrier.

Once back in Nome, Crowley weighed prices he had obtained from the Ferguson brothers for shipping supplies by dog team, against the costs of the plane. It was four cents per pound cheaper by air than the dog team rate of twenty cents a pound. This was a small saving, but in view of the fact the aircraft was also faster, he was inclined to favour the plane.

With the approach of summer, Bahr decided to

split the herd into two groups. The deer would be easier to manage, he speculated, and less likely to stampede. Retaining half the herd at the main camp on the Hunt, he shifted the other half to a location thirty miles down the Kobuk. When the ice finally went out on the Kobuk River, the herders patrolled its shores in boats they had built and fitted with outboard motors. In this way the men could discourage the reindeer from swimming the river in a bid to return south to their home range.

The labour of the drovers was relatively uneventful until the sun reached its zenith, when it never set for several months each summer. Then the green grass came in, the muskeg warmed, and swarms of mosquitoes, one of the great nuisances of the north country emerged. Both men and beasts were forced to alter their habits. The herders' choice was to either find a breezy place to camp, or build a smudge fire — always primed — to fend off the voracious insects. In travelling across country, it was necessary for the herders to remain perpetually in motion or the pests would settle on them like some sort of nightmarish, animated blanket.

There are several varieties of the pest. The first to appear were *Culiseta alaskaensis* Ludlow and *Culiseta impatiens* Walker, which were so eager to get at man and beast they poked their way right up through snow patches and were nicknamed "snow mosquitoes". They were often described by Alaskans, half in jest, as wearing fur coats. Another, even more bloodthirsty species called *Aedes punctodes* Dyar that hatched in late June, could attack in such large swarms that it could kill an animal from loss of blood.

Shepherds in 1930 had no effective repellent against the insidious attacks of the minuscule predators. The men draped nets over their heads, and though effective, the screen was uncomfortable on hot days. The insects were especially annoying during meals. The men wore their headnets while they ate, which made the entire procedure quite awkward. Even frying pans were not immune to the raids. The persistent mosquitoes swarmed onto the hot griddle and sizzled, forming a crust on the food.

In addition to mosquitoes, the deer were susceptible to the warble fly. The flies deposited their eggs on the hair of the deer, usually when the animals were lying down. When the eggs hatched the larvae bored their way through the skin, and worked their way around to come back out the next summer and fall to the ground as pupa. Sores up to six inches across could develop when the deer bit the affected area. Fawns and yearlings were more susceptible to warble flies than older animals, which seemed to acquire an immunity to the fly as they aged.

Yet another insect bothered the deer even more. This was the nostril fly. Shaped like a beetle, the *boaro* as the Lapps called it, hovered level with the snouts of the animals, then attacked them to deposit wiggling larvae in the nasal opening. This sent the animals into shock, and induced muscular convulsions. Usually these contractions passed quickly; but the larvae commenced working their way to the entrance of the throat, where they germinated until the next summer. The grubs became active as they matured, causing the deer to cough and sneeze as they tried to dislodge them. When the larvae ultimately fell to the ground they were often glazed with blood. Reindeer could lose up to a quart of blood a day to insects in a bad year.

The restlessness of the tortured reindeer, coupled with the yearning to return to the home range, was accentuated by their addiction to mushrooms. If a whiff of the spore came to their sensitive noses, they would stampede pell-mell in the direction of the source. The fungi were simply irresistible to the animals.

As bad as conditions were on the Kobuk, the drovers were forced by circumstances to stay where they were for the entire summer. The herd could not be driven toward its ultimate destination on the Mackenzie because there had to be snow over which the supply sleds could be drawn. Also, until the ground was frozen, the men could not travel afoot across the vast swamps of the tundra.

Not all of the hours and days of herding reindeer were wrapped in misery. There was a certain dignity to being a herdsman that set him apart from the average man. A shepherd had to be able to withstand long periods of time alone. In adjusting to this solitary existence, he either achieved a certain level of adaptability and self-reliance that instilled in him the peace of mind to keep going, or he left; it was as simple as that.

There were compensating lures for those who enjoyed the solitary pursuit. A cool wind in summer could present the herder with an opportunity to relax at some pleasant camping place to brew tea or soup while, at the same time, enjoying the spectacular panorama of the nearby mountains. Anyone who toted some sort of a rod could catch fish like Arctic grayling, which were lively fighters, beautiful to look at with their purple sheen, and good to eat. Or by looking skywards, one could derive pleasure from a soaring eagle, the efficient glide of a hawk, and the amusing acrobatics of a raven.

The Lomen reindeer were pastured in one of the most archaeologically-rich regions of North America. This was near Portage, a trail across a neck of the Kobuk. Antler- and stone-tipped spears, stone knives, and cleavers were occasionally kicked up at campfire sites. These signalled a level of culture never observed or even heard of by the men who found them. Cuttings were often seen that could only have been made with stone axes, piquing the curiosity of the lonely herder as he tended the deer.

Nor was life in camp complete drudgery. There, after a long shift spent with the deer, the men converged for steaming hot coffee, and talk, and whittled figurines out of wood and antlers. A herder was his own boss when he was in the field. The logistics of his occupation made it impossible for someone to look over his shoulder every minute in order to tell him what to do. The decisions of the moment were his to make, for better or for worse.

Ivar West was a man who enjoyed being alone. He, too, had come from Norway as had Bahr and Nilluka. He had been chosen for the drive because of his extensive experience, judgement, and ability to apply innovative solutions to unexpected problems that arose. West was alone one day eyeing the fractious, mosquito-crazed segment of the herd he had been assigned to watch along the north bank of the Kobuk, when his charges suddenly bolted into the river and swam across, heading toward their home range. Ivar reacted immediately. He shoved a log into the water and using a piece of driftwood for a paddle, launched the makeshift craft into the swift current. He paddled downstream, angling the log with the flow of the river, and finally reached the opposite shore.

West emerged dripping wet and commenced to run after the deer, but a man on foot was no match for the reindeer. West finally gave up and recrossed the Kobuk. He figured he had lost between three hundred and five hundred deer. However, this was not a devastating setback in view of the fact that with the large fawn crop, the herd had increased in size to five thousand deer.

The disappearance of Ivar's group underlined the problem of watching the deer. One minute a man could be comfortably watching a herd worth one hundred thousand dollars and the next, vainly striving to find its remnants.

Several new crew members were gradually assimilated as the summer wore on. Tom and Peter Wood, two Eskimo brothers, had been hired about the time of Crowley's visit. Edwin Allen, an Eskimo lad from Kobuk, was the last to join. Inuit and Lapps switched back and forth from one tongue to the other as they swapped stories or traded tips. The Inuit deferred to the "working language" of the Laplanders when they discussed subjects that concerned the drive. When outsiders were present, all of the herders conversed in English.

But when it came to disputes, even the same ethnic background did not guarantee there would be no arguments. At times, Bahr's fellow Lapp, Mike Nilluka, who had been in the reindeer industry for almost as long as his boss, was prone to question Bahr's way of doing things and to usurp Andrew's authority. It would take a rare combination of diplomacy and blunt authoritarianism to solve the many inter-personal problems before the drive was over. Carl Lomen, visiting Nome from his usual base in Seattle, heard about the ruckus between Bahr and Nilluka and wrote to Nilluka:

"An expedition like this," Lomen said, "can only have one head, and that head is Andrew. Take your orders from Andrew and pass on to the others only such orders as Andrew gives."[2] Lomen added that he had complete confidence in Nilluka and stated when Andrew Bahr put him in charge of a job he would be the boss of that particular work.

Mike responded immediately with a letter of his own that explained his worries:

"I heard your people were talking to fire me. I did not know why, but I thought folks' reports, so I felt downhearted and sorry. Look like to me that time that our friendship ceases."[3]

Nilluka admitted he and Andrew sometimes had their differences but that they got along all right otherwise. He appreciated Lomen's letter and figured it settled the problem.

As summer waned and the day was fast approaching when the trail drive would resume, Dan Crowley was asked by the Lomens to visit Bahr to make sure all of his plans were in place. This time Crowley travelled to Bahr's camp by boat from Kotzebue via the Kobuk. He was impressed by the beauty of the river as it unwound before him like an exotic, indigo snake.

> The banks are lined with willows and alders and underbrush and . . . the foliage was taking on those lovely autumn shades and presented a gorgeous appearance. The river is quite crooked . . . but every bend unfolds a beautiful picture different from the last . . . We passed many Indian [Eskimo] fishing camps along the river, and they surely are

> picturesque. The white tents setting back among the willows and trees. The racks of hanging fish, the nets hung up to dry, and the boats moored to the bank created a pretty scene.[4]

Dan Crowley reached Bahr's camp the third week of September. Ice was already forming on the river, and the distant hills glistened under newly fallen snow. Freeze-up was near.

Crowley observed that Bahr had things well in hand, despite the many personnel troubles of the summer. The Lapp told Crowley he had assembled five thousand pounds of supplies and equipment for the expedition at the junction of the Ambler and Redstone rivers. And Crowley advised Bahr that they still intended to ferry supplies across the Brooks Range by plane.

The Second Year

CHAPTER 7

Across the Mountains

Crowley returned to Elephant Point while Bahr confronted the details of bringing the reindeer together prior to crossing the Brooks Range. Herders were bivouacked by now in four camps, tending three different bands scattered for sixty miles along the Kobuk River, and a supply camp farther north. By mid-October, the ground had frozen, and the insect hordes had long since disappeared. Rut was still in progress. The bulls over two years old fought for their harems, then serviced up to fifteen females, and sometimes more. Consequently, Bahr held the drive until November, when the mating season was over, and then issued orders to round up the herd.

Only two more steps were required before the drive was resumed. The fawn crop had raised the number of deer to five thousand, but because the contract called for delivery of only three thousand head, the Lomens saw no need to drive the whole herd to Canada. Therefore, two thousand animals were culled and sent back to Naboktoolik. The other step was to fly the supplies to the north slope of the Brooks Range.

When the herd was ready, Bahr sent a wireless message by way of the Fergusons in Shungnak, informing Alfred Lomen in Nome. Lomen hired pilot Sanis E. Robbins for the job of hauling the supplies. Robbins flew north in a Fairchild, picking up Crowley at his headquarters at Elephant Point, then flying on to the Hunt River where they landed on November 19. The destination of the supply flight was the Etivluk River, which Crowley and Bahr had scouted on the earlier excursion.

Bahr hopped aboard the plane and they flew to the cache at the junction of the Ambler and Redstone rivers. Here, they loaded up the plane with a half ton of supplies and headed north. The weather on the Kobuk side of the first range of mountains was clear but changed for the worse after they crossed the spires separating the Kobuk and the Noatak. In spite of this, Robbins managed to spot the Aniuk and flew up the valley in hopes of crossing Howard Pass to the Etivluk. A blizzard farther up the river forced the pilot to retreat the way he had come. Rather than tote the burden of supplies all of the way back to the point of take-off, Crowley told the pilot to land on a lake they discerned near the confluence of the Aniuk and the Noatak. The supplies were unloaded here, but Crowley was reminded again of how easily the weather could sock in a plane. The cost of flying back and forth would be prohibitive, so Crowley decided to haul the remaining two tons of provisions and gear by dog team after all; it appeared to be the only practical way of guaranteeing the shipments would reach the Etivluk River. He hired the Ferguson brothers to begin the tremendous task of sledding the loads across the two mountain ranges. The five five-dog teams employed by Warren and Archie Ferguson were made up of big, tough Malemutes. The animals were not speedsters, but they were capable of performing well in an era which saw the airplane and dog team vying for supremacy of the long-range freight haul. The distance to the Etivluk was 125 miles by air, but considerably longer on the ground. The Fergusons took the job at twenty cents a pound, the price they had quoted earlier.

Oddly enough, *good* weather stymied the drive on the west side of the Hunt. No snow had fallen in the valleys, which meant the Hunt River, though frozen, was a wide expanse of glare ice. To the deer, it looked like newly frozen ice, and they would not venture onto it. Instinctively, the animals knew if they lost their footing they were vulnerable to predators. The men and deer waited for snow.

The herdsmen anxiously scanned the skies while they kept a close watch on the nervous reindeer. They could not afford to let the deer take off in a stampede at this time when the drive was about to resume. Finally, enough snow fell to coat the glare ice, giving sufficient traction for the deer. The blessing of this turn of events brought its own hex in that it did not *stop* snowing as the herd crossed the Hunt and wound its way up the north side of the Kobuk. The drive traversed Jade Creek (the site of one of the largest jade deposits in North America) and reached the banks of the Redstone River.

The mantle of snow became so deep the fawns could not paw their way through it to feed. Even worse, when they did scrape away the snow cover, there was no forage. Bahr wrote: ". . . this country is very poor feeding for deer. Very little reindeer moss. Nothing but brown moss [house moss]."[1]

The snow continued to fall, and the combination of deep snow and poor feed was so calamitous many fawns collapsed and died; upwards of 100 newborn were lost as the herd plodded up the Redstone.

Bahr had not expected to enjoy ideal conditions when afoot or on skis in the Arctic, but it seemed as though his luck was on a permanent holiday. When the storm finally let up, the temperature plummeted to fifty below zero Fahrenheit, and produced eerie results. Heat from the bodies of the bunched animals at this temperature created a fog so thick it blotted out the sight of the herd from the men trying to drive it. A poetic observer might have imagined the scene as a mile-long, rusty-brown dragon breathing out smoke as it slithered by in the snow. The men, deer, and dogs were so glazed with snow crystals they took on the appearance of grim caricatures of a Christmas card.

Peter Wood, because of his astute knowledge of the region, was selected by Bahr to be the guide and replaced Nilluka. Subsequent gripes by Mike indicated that he may not have been happy with this change. Wood forged ahead, testing the ground for lichens and doing his best to point the herd into areas he judged to be sufficient for forage. However, he had mixed success.

Peter and his brother, Tommy, were dependable men, making their way through life by hard work, abstemiousness, and thrift. Peter's history was representative of both — he was born at Shungnak in 1885. His first encounter with reindeer was fifteen years later, when a herd under supervision of the United States Bureau of Education passed by southeast of his home on the way to pasture land on the Koyukuk River.

A year later a government school was built at Shungnak. Peter attended it for two years, then undertook other pursuits. His first job with reindeer came at Kotzebue when he was employed by missionaries in 1907, under Alfred Nilima's supervision. After working one year under a bonus arrangement, Peter was given three deer. By 1911, he had built up his herd to forty-five reindeer.

Peter hired relatives to look after his tiny herd as he sought additional funds working for others. In

1915, he signed on with the Lomen brothers for fifty dollars a month.

Always a frugal man, Peter saved his money. He quit his job with the Lomens in 1918 and purchased a riverboat which he used to operate a freight business out of Selawik, where his parents lived. In winter, he trapped. His herd grew until it numbered several hundred by 1929. That year Bahr and Crowley approached Peter and his brother, Tommy, seeking their services for the drive to Canada, but they had already committed themselves to a prospecting contract. After completing that job, they joined Bahr on the Kobuk.

The success of the Wood brothers in adjusting to another culture, their ability to bend with it and to weave in the threads of their own lifestyle and to do this in a positive, progressive manner was due, in part, to a gifted seer named Maniilaq.

This man was a visionary. He was born on the upper reaches of the Kobuk around the beginning of the 19th century. He foresaw the coming of a new race to the area and that amazing changes would be imparted as a result. He predicted that men would fly on iron sleds and speak through the air over long distances. He prophesied that men would write on thin birch bark. In his own way, Maniilaq, travelling throughout the region, attempted to prepare his people for the huge changes he predicted would come, and in so doing he challenged old taboos that he felt were impediments in his people's way of life. One fear, then widely held, was that if a person processed a caribou skin during fishing season, he would die. The visionary deliberately broke this rule and survived. He also ate beluga meat along with berries, thus defying yet another taboo, and lived through that desecration — the mixture of sea and land foods.

Maniilaq predicted that the arrival of the white man would change these old taboos, and in this way prepared the people for the eventuality. Therefore, when it finally did happen, his thoughts were remembered by some and the cultural shock lessened to that extent. Men like the Wood brothers were able to do individually what cultures as a whole have always done: to borrow from each other, adapt, and combine elements of two different societies.

The drive was plagued with difficulties while ascending the Redstone. Deer fell, spread-eagled on the slippery surface of tiny, wind-whipped glaciers that built up along the creek. The herders quickly propped them back up and led them to a firm surface. Fawns became so deeply buried in the snow they had to be plucked aloft and deposited on sleds. The men suffered also. They slipped on overflows that oozed out of hidden springs to make the ice slick as if greased. They fell into slush ice. Hypothermia, cramps, croup, frostbite, and lack of sleep sapped their strength as they pushed the herd across the divide to enter the valley of the Noatak

River. The debilitating journey had taken a month, twice as long as Bahr had estimated. There was some griping because of it. Bahr wrote in his January report to Lomen: "Some of the boys been very cranky."

Because of the delays, there was no time for tarrying at the Noatak. Bahr was bound and determined to get to the coast of the Arctic Ocean by summer, and already he was behind schedule. The Lapp and his crew pushed the deer twenty miles to the Aniuk River, the artery they would follow across the mountains to the north slope. They crept up this tributary of the Noatak in an almost timid approach to the wind-hammered Howard Pass, the gap through the second mountain range. Trappers who had traversed this route in winter were not encouraging on the prospects of driving a reindeer herd through it. Though comparatively low and wide, the pass was a natural funnel for devastating zephyrs that howled down from the Arctic Ocean, and were sucked through the niche in the Brooks Range by variations of air pressure.

As if on cue, a blizzard ripped through the herd as it approached the pass. The wind swirled among the ranks of men and beasts alike for three long days, threatening to break up the drive. Bahr and his men fanned out on either side of the reindeer herd to make doubly sure it did not reverse directions under the onslaught of the polar blasts. The entourage tended to close up as the deer bucked the fury of the wind. It was an odd way to spend

Christmas, 1930, with Bahr, sometimes known as "The Arctic Moses", leading animals symbolic of the celebration that observed the birth of Christ.

Peter Wood, on skis, led the way into Howard Pass, with Bahr behind him coaxing a double team of sled deer as an enticement to the herd that trailed behind. On the flanks of the line walked Sam Segeok and Theodore Kingeak, who had rejoined the drive after spending most of the summer at their homes. (They had apparently settled their salary problems.) Edwin Allen, proving very dependable, was farther back, as was Tommy Wood, Peter's younger brother, trailwise and tough. Bringing up the drag and escorting the sled deer were Nilluka and West. Assisting them was another Lapp, Tom Nakkala, who was wracked with coughing spells brought on by an attack of pleurisy. The Fergusons' five dog teams and their mushers brought up the rear — the dogs hauling heavy loads characteristic of the Malemute strain. Andrew Bango, and another Lapp, Johnny Rouna, who had pitched in temporarily, decided to leave the drive before reaching the mountains.

As the storm raged, the drivers were lucky if they could proceed for four hours out of every day. Whipped by driven snow, the sled deer's eyes had to be cleared of frozen rime repeatedly before they could go on. Men vigorously rubbed their faces to prevent frostbite. Battered by the wind that spilled over Howard Pass in an unceasing assault, the herdsmen finally reached the north end of the notch. They needed no orders to push the reindeer herd quickly down the treeless far slope to the meagre sanctuary of the valley of the Etivluk.

Bahr and his men made camp, putting up a single tent as a refuge from the wind. The trail boss rotated reliefs, keeping most of the men posted around the herd. He could not afford to lose the deer if, by some surge of adrenalin, the animals suddenly mustered a hidden reserve of strength to bolt back from this unfamiliar territory.

That night Bahr completed a four-page letter he had begun writing in the pass while waiting for the dog teams to catch up with the herd. He gave an account of the ordeal of the pass, and finished the letter in time to post it with the dog mushers deadheading back to the Kobuk. Bahr's link with the outside world was now cut. The trail boss and his men were perched on a brink of the planet that was unmapped, and virtually untravelled by humans. Once he plunged into this trackless waste, Bahr could expect no supplies until he reached the shores of the Arctic Ocean. There would be no turning back for the members of the crew unless they chose to risk crossing the Brooks Range alone in the dead of the winter.

Bahr faced the same problems that had plagued him the first winter. Inevitably, every time a positive factor entered the picture, it was followed by a negative one. In this case, as the drive threaded its way down from the mountains, there was little forage, and no trees to supply firewood. Without forage, the reindeer were increasingly restive and vulnerable to stampeding; and without wood to build fires, the men suffered much from the cold.

The temperature plunged to sixty-five below, making it impossible to move the herd more than a few miles a day, and as the drovers battled the cold, its omnipotence ordained Bahr's every thought. Travails of leadership, accentuated by problems of bitter conditions, began to tug at Bahr from all sides. His countrymen continued to chaff over his strategy to push the reindeer rather than to coax them along with sledders as forerunners. In addition, West, Nilluka, and Nakkala were disturbed because Bahr would not give the herd a mid-day break. They claimed Bahr's failure to order such a rest period weakened the deer.

Peter and Tommy Wood were turning out to be superlative workers as far as Bahr was concerned, yet Tommy irritated Andrew because he kept pestering the trail boss to have his family join him. Bahr wrote: "Thom Wood is mighty good man, but he don't want to stay if family is not along, but he got big family that will be too much bother for us."

Much of Bahr's judgement was now predicated on fear: fear of the unknown, and fear of obstacles that could be flung at him from unexpected sources. These, in turn, invoked the need for either lightning-quick decisions, or those requiring solemn judgement and long-range planning.

The trail boss and his men had to almost literally feel their way along the Etivluk, broaching the ever-present pall of fog created by the body heat of the herd. The cold settled on the men like an invisible strait-jacket, crimping their efficiency until every chore took ten times the normal effort.

The bitter cold was all-pervasive in its influence. It dictated the clothes a man wore. It decreed what he would carry with him. It commanded where and how far he would go. It prescribed how long he would be gone. It directed the use and care of his equipment. Deadening cold was exactly that: it numbed exposed flesh, it stopped the flow of water, it petrified wood, it encumbered the movement of animals.

The more prolonged the cold, the more depressing it was. Bahr was as much subjected to its effects as anyone else, but still was forced to render decisions. He set up the work schedule whereby he dispatched men to keep watch on the herd during the nights when the mercury hit rock bottom and gelid conditions were at their worst. Bahr's most constant fear, day-in and day-out, was that a caribou herd would trek past his animals and draw them off into the snow-shrouded hills.

The herd dogs at such times were indispensable for staving off inroads of caribou. The dogs were the eyes, ears, and nose of the herders in the long darkness of the winter's night, and they were the drovers' legs during the short twilight of the Arctic day. Without canines to make the men aware, bands of caribou that numbered up to twenty thousand could quickly envelop and absorb the reindeer herd as they passed by. Even with his knowledge of the dogs' capabilities, it was difficult for Bahr to shake this worry that plagued him day and night. One pass, and all would be lost.

Bahr strived to conserve rations as the expedition progressed down the Etivluk. The colder the weather, the more food the men needed. This was a natural result of the basic requirements needed to sustain life itself. Low temperatures meant the body demanded that much more fuel to maintain its basic ninety-eight degrees of warmth. Since Bahr had absolutely no indication of when he would again receive supplies, he was forced to ration food in anticipation that he might not be able to restock the larder until he reached the Arctic Ocean. And in so doing he further aggravated the drovers.

A trail drive, like an army, travels "on its stomach", and a leader such as Bahr felt the pressure when his men were not getting what they considered to be proper food. Not only was there not enough of the staples, but Bahr had taken it upon himself to be the chef. With the limited fuel along the Etivluk, most of the food was only half-cooked, and definitely not conducive either to good digestion or high morale.

Bahr was accustomed to rough fare, as were the drovers. However, they were not as stoic about it as he was. The gripes of the men had just started to peak in intensity when relief was accorded by improved conditions. The herdsmen began to spot and cut alder, willow, and cottonwood as they worked their way down from the lofty highlands of the Brooks Range. It took them a month to reach the Colville River from the pass. They proceeded along the larger river, which flowed directly east parallel to the Brooks Range. Here pieces of driftwood were seen poking up through the snow. The men sequestered these scraps and sticks in their packs during the day and brought them to camp at night. Consequently, along with wood cut for the purpose, they could build a fire intense enough to cook *hot* meals and produce enough heat to dry out their clothes.

February 1931 arrived with Bahr's ice-encrusted group toiling resolutely along the Colville. Their slow progress caused Bahr to fret over yet another problem: the female deer were pregnant and he could foresee that his goal of reaching the Arctic Coast by fawning time was fast slipping away.

The expedition bucked the elements along the river for the entire month of February before a break came. An airplane, seemingly coming in from nowhere, landed almost at Bahr's feet on March 9. Pilot Joe Crosson had been on a mercy flight carrying diphtheria anti-toxin north to Barrow when he spotted the herd. When he reached Barrow, he wired Alfred Lomen and asked him if he could be of any assistance while he was in the area. Lomen wired back that he would pay $300 for a letter from Bahr.

Crosson would have done the favour for free, but when he stopped to consider the risk of landing his plane where the dangers of ice hummocks or overflow might go unnoticed until it was too late, he accepted Lomen's generous offer. The pilot found the trail of the herd on his return flight. He followed it for forty miles in a northeasterly direction along the Colville before he sighted Bahr's camp in a draw opposite the mouth of the Killik, a tributary of the larger river, and landed.

The first words of the herders who approached him were to ask for more food. Tommy Wood said: "We are out of everything except coffee and fruit. We must have grub soon."

Bahr soon snowshoed up to join the others and Crosson explained his mission. He told the foreman the Lomens wanted a personal note from him as to what his needs were, if any. The pilot waited for about ten minutes while Bahr shuffled the pencil and paper back and forth in his hands, but did not write a word. Since the temperature was forty below zero, the motor of the plane had to be left running, which in turn, was burning up the aviator's precious fuel supply. Crosson told Bahr he had to write something, and walked away from the old-timer, figuring his presence may have been intimidating the Lapp. Bahr fumbled around and at last scribbled a short note and handed it to Crosson, unfinished. It read:

> Dear Alfred I am in a hurry We are here now
> at the Burning coal mine our herd are all play
> out has been not much feed no mos[s] but I
> don't know farther down. We would like

> mak[e] Kubarok [Kuparuk] on the coast this spring if can We would need grub to be landet to mouth of Colville or to Kobaruk on the coast but we get not cha[n]ce to get our selves. You have to see where and how you get us groub for whole summer and landit to East side of Colville mouth Kubaruk we had
>
> [A. Bahr][2]

The pilot snatched the note from Bahr's hands on the run and took off with barely enough gas to return to his company's fuel cache at Bettles on the way to Fairbanks.

During the month following Crosson's visit, the drive maintained its slogging pace to reach the junction of the Anaktuvuk and Colville rivers on April 1. Bahr ordered a halt and decided to make camp for a much needed rest while he pondered the future. He was seventy-five miles from the mouth of the Colville River where it drained into the Arctic Ocean. Fawning season was only a few weeks away. The trail boss knew that once that occurred the drive would be stalled for almost two months until the young ones were strong enough to travel. Bahr calculated he would rest briefly before pushing the heavily laden females as far as he dared before the fawns came.

The Fairbanks manager of the company that employed Crosson, Pacific Alaska Airlines, wired

Alfred Lomen who at that time was in Juneau serving as a legislator in the Alaskan territorial government. He advised Alfred about the pilot's visit to Bahr, and quoted the Lapp's needs, which were unspecific other than that he wanted "grub".

Alfred Lomen's expertise was being sought more and more by Bahr as the drive continued. The reason for this was that Alfred, for all intents and purposes, was now running the Alaskan part of the reindeer operation. He, like his brothers, was born in Minnesota where he had been a remarkable athlete in both baseball and basketball. He moved to Nome with his parents, where he became manager of the Nome *Gold Digger* newspaper. He also attended photography school for a year, and then joined up with Ralph and Harry in a combined drug store and photographic studio they opened in Nome.

Alfred was involved in the Lomen reindeer operation from its outset. He thoroughly learned all aspects of the business, from herding to butchering the animals. And though his election to the territorial house took him away from the firm for a part of the year, he retained his supervisory ties.

On receiving the wire from Fairbanks, Alfred relayed the request to Dan Crowley in Nome and asked him to take care of Bahr's wants. Being familiar with the drive's original manifest of supplies, Crowley made mental evaluations of what the men might need, and acted accordingly. He journeyed to Fairbanks where he arranged for a plane and the same pilot to fly back to the drive. Dan assembled the usual staples such as flour, canned milk, coffee, tea, baking powder and soda, sugar, salt, and canned vegetables and fruit, which, to save weight, he removed from boxes and repacked in sacks. Even then the total added up to one thousand pounds.

Crowley and Crosson took off from Fairbanks on April 9. The pilot had last visited the herd a month earlier, so he realized that a considerable amount of guesswork would be required to figure out its location now. Crosson put the plane down at Bettles after a two-hour flight and topped up the fuel tanks. He took off again and followed the John River to its headwaters.

The John issued forth from the Endicott Mountains, a rugged barrier that made up a part of the Brooks Range. A heavy layer of clouds embraced the mountain tops and held Crosson below four thousand feet. Undeterred by this difficulty, the pilot navigated through a maze of canyons and peaks, and passed over a low divide to the headwaters of the Anaktuvuk River. The low ceiling continued to inhibit the flight as they flew north toward the Colville. Finally, the clouds dissipated over the northern plain. Bright sunshine smiled down and the land beneath sparkled under its rays. Soon they spotted caribou tracks, and then caribou, but no reindeer. Crowley was able to distinguish between the two animals from the air by the tracks they made. Caribou were free-wheeling and were widely spread out, whereas the reindeer herd was bunched up and would often as not show ski tracks next to it.

Based on the number of days since Crosson had visited the drive and the average miles-per-day a herd that size could travel, Crowley estimated that they would find the reindeer about forty miles down the Colville from where Crosson had last seen them. Crosson used Crowley's rough calculations as a guide and cut straight across to the Colville from the Anaktuvuk. He gambled on saving a few miles, and precious fuel. The attempt was a worthy one, but as is often the case with a gamble, it was unsuccessful. There was no camp, or reindeer, in sight. The frustrating question that now faced them was which way to turn: up or down the Colville? Crosson left the decision up to Crowley; as far as Crossen was concerned, he could burn just so much fuel and no more. When the gas gauge reached a certain level, he would have to turn back, no matter what his client wanted. There was no room for a miscalculation.

Dan did some quick figuring and told the pilot to follow the Colville upstream to the point where he had landed a month earlier. They proceeded as slowly as the plane could fly in order to save fuel and found the campsite vacated.

Crowley was now faced with yet another decision. Should they retrace their flight down the Colville or turn around and fly northeast, cutting off an elbow of the river in hopes they would pick up the herd farther down? Dan decided to stay with the river. Crosson would let him know the limits of the fuel.

Crowley fretted, wondering if he had missed the reindeer. From the air they looked like caribou, but their tracks would not lie. Scanning the valley floor, Crowley told the pilot to fly down the Colville as far as he dared. Crowley later wrote: "Having gone seventy-five miles downriver, we picked up the trail. It resembled a white ribbon winding along the river. Now down on the river and then up on the bank, as the deer left the river to feed on the moss which grows along the banks."[3]

A few minutes after spotting the tracks, they saw the herd on a small creek about a mile from the Colville. Next, three tents pitched at the mouth of the Anaktuvuk came into view. Three reindeer sleds left no doubt about whom the tents belonged to. The pilot made a perfect landing on the Colville, coming to a stop right in front of the camp. It was ten o'clock in the morning, or five hours and forty-five minutes out of Fairbanks.

Six hours of daylight were required for the return flight. Since the days were already quite long, this afforded Crowley enough time to learn from Bahr his plans with regards to the coming summer. There was no telling when contact with the drive would next be made, although the Lomens had agreed to supply the men by plane if it had to be done that way. The expense for this was high, and the drive could not incur costs unendingly if the project was to remain profitable. Canada had made good on its second payment of eighty-two thousand dollars but the longer the herd was in the field, the heavier was the drain on the company's coffers.

While the crew unloaded the supplies from the plane, Crowley and Bahr adjourned to a tent for tea. The Lapp gave his visitor a rundown on the progress of the drive. He said the herd could cover only a few miles a day at best, and on some days did not gain an inch. He reassured Crowley that he would reach the Arctic coast within three or four months, even if he had to push the deer in the summer to do it. Once there, he intended to purchase enough supplies from local traders to hold over the expedition until the ice went out and trading vessels appeared.

Crowley discovered the crew was not so short of grub as he had been led to believe from the tone of the earlier airplane message. Bahr told him he had carefully rationed the food, particularly the staples. This meant there was enough left to last another month without Crowley's additions. Also, three moose had been killed only the day before his arrival, so the drive was well stocked with meat.

However, even the moose meat and the food brought in by Crowley did nothing to assuage the declining morale of the herdsmen, who continued to gripe about their situation. In his report to Alfred Lomen, Crowley said: ". . . Andrew confided to me that he was much dissatisfied with Nilluka and West and would discharge them if he could get men to take their places."

Dan Crowley did not hear any complaints directly from the men, but Bahr was with him most of the time, making it difficult for them to speak freely. When it came time for him to leave, just as Crowley was about to step onto the plane, Tom Nakkala, one of the Lapp herders, stepped forward. Citing ill health, he asked to go back with the plane. This was all right with Bahr and Crowley, and since the aircraft had been lightened by one thousand pounds, the pilot had no objections. Once Nakkala was aboard and the plane had taken off, he spoke his mind about Bahr's handling of the herd. His complaints reflected the thinking of the other Lapps, West and Nilluka, with a few more gripes added to the original ones. Crowley wrote:

> Tom thinks in driving this past winter the deer were pushed too hard at the start. He says as a rule they would commence the drive long before daylight and keep the herd moving until dark, never stopping at noon to allow them to eat. Also the path followed by the deer was not nearly as straight as it would have been if lead deer were used.

Nakkala also complained that the sleds made in Seattle were fifty pounds heavier than those usually crafted by the Lapps, which, he felt, put an abnormal burden on the draft animals.

These factors were partially ascribed by Crowley

as the reasons the drive was behind schedule. The venture was originally estimated to take from eighteen months to two years. It was now April 1931; the drive had been en route for fifteen months and had covered a distance, as a crow flies, of only two hundred and fifty miles. This left Bahr and his men still five hundred air miles short of their destination on the Mackenzie River.

After Dan returned to Fairbanks, he sent his report to Alfred Lomen with an estimate of how much longer the expedition would take. "It is doubtful if the drive can be completed *next* winter," he wrote. The herd he estimated to be at about three thousand deer.

Lomen stoically accepted the fact that the herd would not reach the Mackenzie before the winter of 1932–1933, and forwarded Crowley's sobering observation to Finnie in Canada.

CHAPTER 8

Mutiny

The slow progress of the drive gave the Canadian government more time to build the reindeer station at Kittigazuit.[1] However, the fact that the herd now appeared to be behind schedule was not looked upon with sympathetic eyes by the Porsild brothers. They thought Andy Bahr was deliberately orchestrating the delays to prolong the undertaking so he could accumulate more money by way of his monthly paycheque.

Erling commented in a letter to Finnie: "I feel that Andrew, who is drawing a very good salary, is not too much in a hurry."[2] Bob Porsild echoed his brother's feelings a few weeks later: "No doubt Bahr has had unfortunate working conditions at the beginning of the drive, but on the other hand, 'Lapp politics' show plainly through the whole affair. The whole thing looks rather 'Lappish'."[3] In

Sheldon Jackson College

Sheldon Jackson, an educator in the mold of the great missionary administrators, first conceived the idea of importing reindeer from Siberia to alleviate native starvation.

Lindeberg Family

Jafet Lindeberg, a Norwegian who came to the Yukon during the Klondike gold rush and ended up owning Alaska's largest gold-dredging operation, was a principal backer of the Lomens' reindeer venture.

Archives of the University of Alaska

The Lomen brothers ran by far the largest operation in Alaska for three decades: *standing, left to right*, Harry, Alfred, Mrs. Carl (Laura) Lomen, and Carl; *seated*, their mother, Mrs. G. J. Lomen.

Courtesy Elly Porsild

The two Danish-Canadian brothers who researched and advocated establishing a reindeer herd in Canada to imitate the Alaskan success story: Bob, left, and Erling Porsild.

Richard Finnie

Oswald S. Finnie of the Canadian Department of the Interior, who earned his stripes as a mining-claims administrator during the Klondike gold rush, was the Ottawa mandarin responsible for overseeing the reindeer project.

Drew University Library Archives

Arthur, left, and Leonard Baldwin, New York attorneys with a flair for the unusual, acted as the Lomens' attorneys and intermediaries with the Canadian government.

Public Archives of Canada

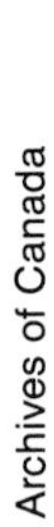

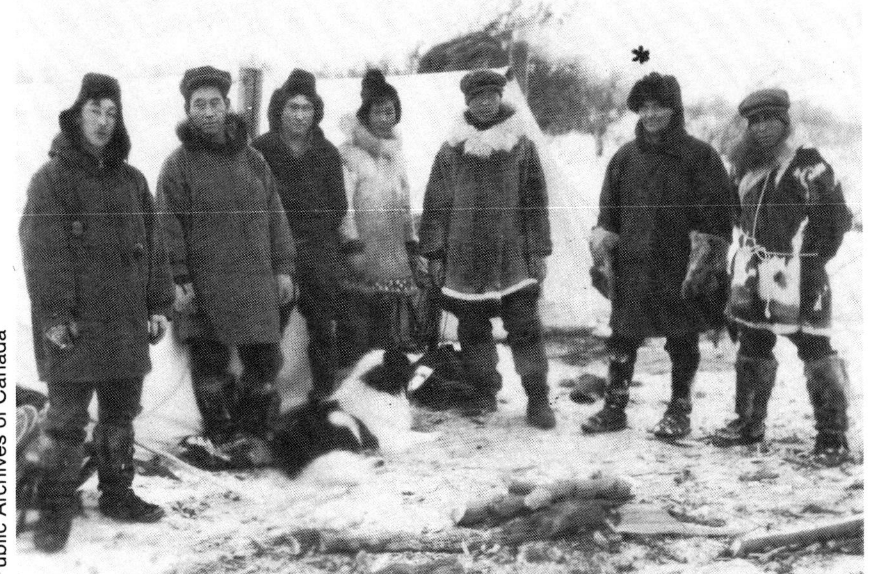

Andrew Bahr (second from right) with five of his reindeer herdsmen: August Ome, Shelby David, David Henry, Sam Segeok, and Theodore Kingeak. The woman in the centre is the wife of one of the Eskimos.

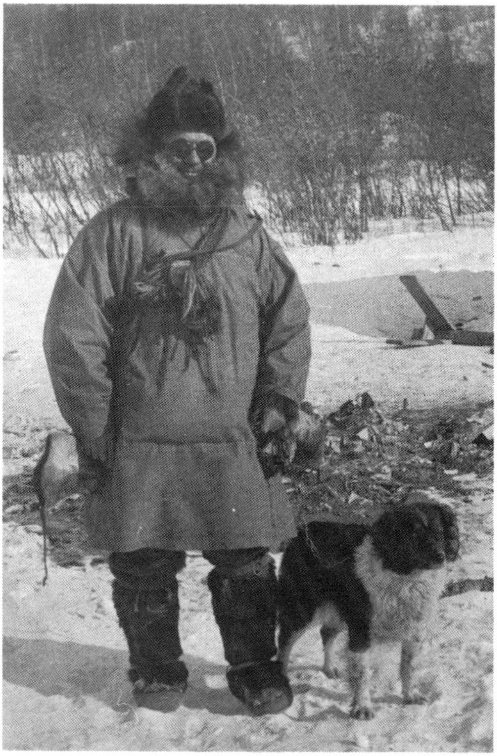

Public Archives of Canada

Andy Bahr earned the nickname "The Arctic Moses" for leading the epic five-year trail drive.

Public Archives of Canada

Public Archives of Canada

Ivar West stares at a stubborn steer while dividing up loads for the sleds along the Colville River.

Public Archives of Canada

Snow house built like a cabin to provide shelter from Arctic gales, on the banks of the Shaviovik River.

Opposite page: Strung out for over half a mile, the herd prepares to cross flare ice on the Kobuk River.

Courtesy Elly Porsild

The first reindeer station at Kooryuak on the lower Mackenzie River.

Courtesy Elly Porsild

Bob Porsild (with cigar), next to his new wife Elly (in a white coat), and Reverend Murray (second from front), after their wedding in Aklavik, NWT, in September 1930. Porsild's assistants Hans Hansen and Wilhelm Hatting are at far right.

Public Archives of Canada

Iron man Edwin Allen leads sled deer across tundra.

Courtesy Elly Porsild

The Lapp families pitched in to help with the fencing at the Mackenzie station. *Front*: Susanna Tornensis, Anna Pulk, baby Ellen with Mikkel Pulk, Louis Brockage, Aslak Tornensis. *Back*: Nels Pulk, Anna Tornensis, Art Pulk, Maria Hatta, Mrs. Erling (Asta) Porsild, Mrs. Bob (Elly) Porsild, Karin Porsild, and Erling Porsild.

Archives of the University of Alaska

Peter and Thomas Wood (second and third from left) were one of four sets of brothers from three different cultures responsible for the ultimate success of the monumental reindeer drive.

Public Archives of Canada

Lassoing sled deer at Kay Point, near the end of the drive. Note the lone man and dog holding the herd on the right while several others work at the left. A temporary camp tent is visible in the centre, just behind the herd.

the same breath, Bob affirmed his faith that Bahr would deliver the herd in good shape and the delay would not affect the quality of the stock.

Neither the Canadian government nor other principals such as the Lomens were at first overly disturbed by the slow progress of the drive. Erling Porsild had suggested earlier that the Lomens should hire a white man (that is, other than Lapp or Eskimo) to work in the field with Bahr ". . . to take care of business aspects of the drive, to oversee employee relations, and to make sure the drive kept on track."[4] However, finding a white experienced enough to go into the field on a venture of that length and nature was not easily done. Anyone qualified for the job could be expected to demand a much higher wage than the Lomens could afford to pay. Even base-wage employees were difficult to hire because trapping at this time generated a higher income. Trappers wanted ten dollars a day to work for Bahr, or three hundred dollars a month, which was two hundred a month more than the Eskimos on the drive were making, and nine hundred dollars more a year than Erling Porsild himself!

Through it all, the Lomens were candid about keeping the Canadian government well informed of the drive's progress. They even adopted Bahr's trail philosophy that he was "making haste slowly".[5] Whether Bahr was fulfilling the actual intent of that maxim was subject to debate. To Erling and Bob, he wasn't making haste, not even slowly!

While Bahr's cranky crew and obstinate reindeer crept, snail-like, across the polar tundra, management on the Canadian side was smitten with problems of its own.

One item that demanded attention was a proviso for taking care of the herd after it was delivered. Finnie had asked the Lomens to furnish someone who would stay on and oversee the deer in Canada. Tommy Wood and his brother, Peter, had promised to take the job, providing they could have their families with them, but the final arrangement was not an absolute certainty. Leonard and Arthur Baldwin, the New York lawyers who had financed the Lomens, suggested to Cory that he also hire carefully selected Lapps directly from Scandinavia for the carry-over period.

Finnie acted on the Baldwins' advice and authorized Erling Porsild to go to Norway to choose herders. He set sail on June 13, 1931. This did not give him much time to hire three Lapps and their families, bring them back by ship to Canada, and then escort them west with the idea of catching the last boat down the Mackenzie River before freeze-up. The responsibility of building living quarters for the Lapp and Inuit families fell to Bob Porsild, who scheduled the summer of 1932 to complete this project.

Finnie had yet another task for Bob. This stemmed from the Lomens' worries over the route the herd would follow across Mackenzie Bay and its islands. No detailed charts were available, so Finnie asked the Surveyor General to draw up a sketch map of the route. Leonard Baldwin, in an Ottawa visit to Cory, had stressed the need for such a map after viewing aerial photos. Finnie selected Bob Porsild to make a reconnaissance. Up to that time, May 1931, the general supposition on the part of the drive's administrators was that Bahr would attempt crossing the bay in the spring of 1932. Crowley's estimate that the drive would be stalled through 1933 had either not yet been received, or if it had been, was overlooked.

A near-fatal accident occurred in June that was to set back Porsild's timetable at the reindeer station for many months. On June 3, he had cleaned out the stove and dumped the ashes off the back porch of the station's main building, which was also his home. Apparently some of them were still alight. A stiff wind fanned the embers and blew them up against the building, setting it afire. Bob and Elly barely escaped with their lives as the two-storey structure went up in flames. The building was completely destroyed, and their losses were heavy. Provisions, bedding, kitchen utensils, tools, firearms, instruments, stationery, and business and personal papers were destroyed. Bob suffered painful burns on his face and hands while attempting to put out the blaze.

The fire interrupted Porsild's schedule, and also caused reverberations elsewhere. Bob wired news of the disaster to Finnie, who advised him the loss would be replaced. The director, in turn, found it necessary to explain the setback to the department's controller, who was already adjusting his budget to provide for hiring the Lapps, and for making a survey of Mackenzie Bay.

Just about all aspects of the reindeer drive at this time were suddenly in a state of suspended animation, with Bob Porsild burnt out and unreachable at his camp, Erling in Europe in search of reindeer personnel, and Andy Bahr somewhere along the Arctic rim engaged in holding a herd of exhausted and starving deer.

It seemed things could not get any worse, but they did.

A week after Crowley left Bahr on the Colville, the Lapp pushed the herd forward again. Bahr changed directions for fear of running into native-owned reindeer herds in the vicinity of the mouth of the Colville. He chose a route that ran diagonally, in a line northeast from the Colville, to cross a tributary, the Itkillik, and another stream farther east, the Kuparuk, with the destination being a trading post situated on an island in the delta of the Saganavirktok River.

Fifty-below-zero temperatures and gale-force winds almost paralyzed the drive between the Colville and the Itkillik rivers, where the drovers met some natives for the first time since crossing the Brooks Range. They were Eskimos that spoke a slightly different dialect than the Kobuk people. Bahr hired three youths at their hunting camp to help his tired crew.

It took Bahr and his men a little over a week to drive the herd to the Itkillik from their Colville River bivouac, a distance of twenty-five miles. By this time the does, heavy with young, were tired out. Bahr knew they had reached the absolute limit of their endurance, and ordered the men to set up a semi-permanent camp for the duration of the fawning season.

The weather jinx that seemed to be riding on Bahr's shoulders continued — prompted by a condition peculiar to the north slope of the Brooks Range, which is actually classified as a desert climate because of its low annual precipitation. In winter, fierce winds pick up snow crystals off the ground giving an illusion of a blizzard, when there is actually no additional snowfall. Fifty feet above the surface the air can be clear and the sun shining, but to the man on foot in the flying snow, it is a brutal storm. The Eskimos call it *natiqviksuk*, or "ground drifting". A vicious ground wind raked the herd just as the fawns began to drop, and continued for a week. Many of the newly born froze to death in their afterbirth. Others that survived the onslaught of the savage Boreas died later because their mothers had little milk due to poor forage in the area. Fawn casualties were fifty per cent — probably over seven hundred died — and losses of does were heavy.[6]

The drovers were not much better off than the deer. They were cold, tired, and irritable. The situation with regards to the camp mess did not help things any. The fact that no cook was hired to care for the wants of the men was a basic oversight on the part of those involved with the drive that would haunt it from start to finish. It all but guaranteed conditions that undermined morale. The Lomens could be blamed as much for leaving too heavy a responsibility in Bahr's hands as the Lapp was in failing to assume it. He could do only so much.

Bahr was usually the cook; if he did not do the job, someone else did, or the men fended for themselves. Breakfast was rolled oats, coffee or tea, and biscuits, baked by Bahr. Seldom was the breakfast menu varied.

The most wholesome of the day's meals was served at three o'clock in the afternoon. This was a mulligan stew composed of the basics of meat and rice, and anything else of nutritional value chucked into the pot. Other staples for lunch were biscuits and tea.

Supper was taken around eight or nine at night and usually consisted of dried fruit, biscuits, and tea. Because the men in the field often pulled twenty-four-hour shifts, they crammed snacks of biscuits and pilot bread into their parkas before going out to join the herd. The menus were monotonous, sometimes tasteless, and often lacked the full range of nutrients.

There was no overlooking how valuable the reindeer dogs were to the drive, and as a consequence, they were fed well, receiving a mash made out of dried fish cooked in rice, cornmeal, or rolled oats.

This was doled out once a day, and varied when a caribou or moose was taken.

Reindeer were not to be killed unless the men were faced with starvation or a deer was injured.

Poor food, extended hours, and unremitting cold resulted in controversy. According to Peter Wood's recollections, most of this originated with Nilluka and West.

The two " . . . put their tent alongside our tent," Wood later told an interviewer. "One Lapp never show up for a whole week. He told Andrew he was quitting work. He put a sign on top of the snow in the river so that a plane could land. He wrote with sand: 'Please land, passenger.' But plane didn't show up."[7]

Because the camp was pegged out at one permanent location, the deer had to be shifted about in order to obtain proper forage. This made it necessary to graze the herd as far as ten miles away from the tent complex. A man scheduled to relieve another was forced to endure a long, tiring trip across the frozen tundra before his watch even began. This meant the individual being replaced could never be sure when his successor would show up. On one occasion, Peter Wood and a companion spent a week and a half on the range. They ran out of grub after two days, and were reduced to subsisting on caribou and ptarmigan until their reliefs finally arrived.

Under these most trying of circumstances, the Wood brothers continued to earn kudos from Bahr in the reports he sent to the Lomens whenever he got the chance: "Mr. Peter Wood is a good man . . . and he got good reindeer dog. These brothers are the best men I got now."[8]

Coming from Bahr, this was the ultimate compliment. It demonstrated that the Wood brothers had mastered all aspects of reindeer herding. That the Inuit brothers could successfully compete in the reindeer industry after having been exposed to the business for only a generation spoke well for the entire reindeer program. Sheldon Jackson's dream had been to give the Eskimo people an occupation they could depend on that approximated a native lifestyle, yet one by which they could compete in a twentieth-century economy. The Wood brothers were solid examples of what could be achieved by a patient, orderly program.

Calving ended in mid-May; and Bahr resolved to stay another month on the Itkillik until the fawns were stronger. Their condition began to improve perceptibly with warmer weather. By the end of May, cracks began to appear in the visage of the north-slope winter: grass hummocks that peeped above their mantle of snow; a first, lone migrating bird that plopped down next to an ice-free eddy of the Itkillik; buds appeared on willow bushes; the royal purple of an emerging crocus stood in sharp contrast to the patch of thawed ground from which it grew. Belly plants such as birches and willows, brothers of more upright flora farther south, began to show above the melting snow. Gradually, patches of brown tundra grass grew larger as the snow dissolved, until one morning the men could look for miles and see a world of tan rather than a world of white.

Andrew Bahr could not stay inland. He realized it was imperative that he shift the deer to the coast, where they could be exposed to the ocean breezes so crucial to their comfort and health. Most of the snow was now gone, and the trail boss knew he must push the herd as far and as quickly as he could in order to gain ground before the tundra turned soft and spongy under the heat of the sun.

Without snow, the sleds were of no more use, and therefore carefully cached pending their use again next fall. Bahr selected Nilluka and West to take on the job of training the sled deer to carry packs. The deer proved to be skittish with the strange weight on their backs, and were difficult to manage. The Lapps cursed the obstinate animals with a talent mule skinners would have envied. Finally, the deer were gentled down as much as could be expected.

Andrew gave the Wood brothers and some of the Eskimos the job of guiding the main herd. The rest, including West and Nilluka, were to escort the pack deer across the Arctic plain. Their progress turned out to be even slower than that of the Eskimos driving the herd.

The drive finally set out for the coast, and already the periods of warmth were so softening the tundra it became difficult to walk through. The men sank knee-deep in the moss carpet as they struggled across it. The deer, on the other hand, more easily traversed the quagmire on their large, splayed hooves.

By now all of the "white man's" staples such as flour and oats were gone and the men were living mostly on caribou meat. Two of the three newly-hired Eskimo youths became thoroughly disillusioned with reindeer herding and quit. Peter Wood recalled: "One of them was so hard up and crying, he wanted to go back. About twenty miles from the fawning place he says he is played out."

The tundra came alive as the exodus of men and deer plodded northwards, and half way to the "Sag" River summer finally broke. Overnight, the grass turned green, and flowers bloomed. Ground squirrels were suddenly seen atop almost every mound. Hyperactive collared lemmings scurried around in profuse numbers, feeding on morsels of sedges and cotton grass.[9] They and ground squirrels, along with voles, mice and hare were staples upon which the predators of the tundra fed. These hunters, too, were visible in the daylight hours of the Arctic. Gray-brown Arctic foxes, having shed their white winter coats, scooted across the savannah, hardly looking up as the reindeer herd snaked its way through their territory. Overhead, hawks, owls, and falcons glided across the expanse of grasslands, their keen eyes alert to any movement that betrayed the presence of a rodent, upon which the raiders would pounce. The barren-ground grizzly was also astir, now out of hibernation, and a nuisance to the herders. A whiff of this largest of North America's land carnivores was enough to evoke a panic among the jittery deer and send them off on a stampede.

The sun hovered above the horizon for the full twenty-four hours of the day. When there were no clouds or wind, the heat became oppressive. The sun's rays thawed the surface of the frozen soil and there emerged an endless network of lakes, bogs, and swamps. It was a collage of land and water resting like a huge birdbath on a rock-hard footing, the giant sea of frozen subsurface ground. Called permafrost, it ranged in depth from hundreds to thousands of feet. It thawed in summer only to a depth of a foot or two, leaving water that had no place to drain because of the solid floor underneath it. This manifestation, which was more prevalent here than on the Kobuk, created an even more ideal breeding ground for mosquitoes.

When the summer hatch spewed forth these insects it spelled torture for man and beast. Their pinpoint stabs drove warm-blooded creatures to distraction. Equally as irritating for the drovers was the noise — the pervasive, infernal drone that never stopped. This whine, which surged in intensity depending on the pressure of the air, was a form of mental torment that seemed to demand universal repentance from those who dared to challenge the polar tundra.

The mosquito menace plagued the dogs and the

deer, but the dogs suffered more because their snouts were so close to the ground. The side of their muzzles often dripped with blood from the attacks of the voracious insects; the tips of the canines' noses were churned a raw pink from the unceasing bites of the mosquitoes.

As the men escorted the herd through the wetness of the tundra, mosquitoes rose up in swarms to hover over the men and deer. The insects were like some weird inverse shadow, reflecting the flock's every move. On clear, windless days, the herd could be spotted from many miles off by the whirling cloud above it.

The drive crossed the Kuparuk, two-thirds of the way to their summer destination. Then a large band of caribou galloped through the protective screen of dogs and men to draw off over one hundred deer before the gap was closed. Such incursions slowed down the herd, but the men with the pack deer were doing even worse. Ivar West, struggling to lead three deer loaded with guns and ammunition, was subjected to a climatic flip-flop when a dense fog swirled inland from the coast to suddenly envelop his position. Unable to see his way, West figured the best thing to do was to remain right where he was and wait for the weather to clear. He carefully cropped a trio of grass hummocks and tied the deer to them. He then wrapped himself in a ground sheet and took a nap. Several hours went by when a sense of movement woke up the Lapp in time to see the rumps of his deer disappear into the murk behind a dozen caribou.

West cursed the Lapp trickster gods and promptly set off after the three vagrants. He was without a gun, food, or any other essential for survival. The Lapp tramped for about an hour when he realized the search was futile, so he sat down and waited for the fog to lift. The hours dragged by for perhaps an entire day, he was not sure. When the fog finally lifted, he hiked northeastwards as Bahr had advised his men to do if they became separated from the main herd. West intuitively calculated where the herd might be and kept walking. Only one who had spent many years wandering the vast plains of the North, like Ivar, would have possessed the self-confidence to continue since his compass was of no help in finding the elusive, ever-moving herd.

West's trek into the subjective continued for ten long days. He walked until he could walk no more, his feet having swelled up from continual dousing in the frigid seep of the tundra. Incapacitated by this gout-like condition where the slightest bruise caused infinite pain, West lay down, resigned to the fact that he would die. The next morning his fellow drovers found him, only a short distance from the herd, his dead reckoning having prevailed. The men had to cut the mukluks off his feet, but he was alive.

West was not the only one to lose his way. Mike Nilluka went to sleep in a selected spot of soft mosses only to discover, when he woke up, that the herd had moved on. He spent two days searching for the deer before he eventually found the camp, slightly the worse for wear.

Bahr was not happy with the adventures of his two most experienced men, particularly West's loss of the deer that carried guns and ammunition that were so valuable to the drive. These men were of about the same age as Bahr, but very possibly had not "worn" as well. He was inclined to give them the benefit of the doubt in his dealings with them, but even he had his limitations.

Bahr's troubles seemed never-ending as the drive edged to the northeast. The deer were restless and the men were ornery. Plagued by mosquitoes, relentless sun, limitless swamps, sleet storms that soaked a man and froze his clothes at the same time, lightning bolts that jarred the skies with abrupt ferocity, thunder that rolled like some ethereal battle fought in the heavens, squalls which appeared from nowhere to immerse the drovers, and rivers that ran brimful and suddenly became impassable, Bahr fought to hold the drive together. Despite their best efforts, the drovers still lost about five hundred deer on that forced march to the coast.

Personnel problems became acute, and ironically, continued to come from his own countrymen, Ivar West and Mike Nilluka.[10] Their nagging criticism, carelessness, and lack of loyalty irritated Bahr so much he made up his mind to fire them. However, he was in the unenviable position of not being able to do this. He could order them not to work, but he could not order the two men to refrain from eating food, even though the supplies were virtually nil. Nor could he send them away out of hand, as that would have been the same as imposing a death sentence in that far-off land.

These frustrations pressed Bahr to the limit of his patience. One might wonder why he did not resign himself? However, the fibre of the man was tied up in reindeer and reindeer herding. Bahr was not the type of person inclined to quit a project before it was finished. He needed few incentives other than his own iron will. Possibly this in itself was galling to the men who worked for him, most of them being much younger and less demanding of themselves than Bahr.

The drive arrived at a point twelve miles up the Saganavirktok River from its mouth on July 2, 1931. The reason for Bahr's preoccupation with the "Sag" River was that he knew Jack Smith ran a trading post on Foggy Island, situated in the river's delta. There, Bahr would have access to the store as well as coastwise communications by boat. He hoped that the attitudes of the men would be ameliorated by the improved conditions. In this he was wrong. The discontented herders realized they could now quit and catch a trading vessel home, and they became more impudent than ever. One crewman threatened to expose the fact the herders were shooting caribou and moose out of season when he returned to Nome.

Adding to the adverse developments, and probably the reason for some of them, was a desperate need for food supplies and foot gear.

July 4, 1931, Bahr and Tommy Wood built a boat frame out of willow sticks lashed together with caribou sinew, and stretched a canvas cloth over it. With this makeshift craft, and homemade driftwood paddles, they set off down the fast-flowing "Sag". Several hundred yards along, they found that their untreated canvas leaked so badly they had to run the craft ashore to dump out the water. This was repeated until they reached Foggy Island. There, Bahr found out Smith had neither food nor foot gear for sale.

A man dying of thirst and expecting to find water at an oasis could not have been much worse off than the trail boss. Plainly, Smith's cupboards were bare, the year's first trading vessel not yet having visited the post. Bahr paused to consider the dilemma, then asked Smith if he would take his own seaworthy boat west to the trading post at Beechey Point to fill the order. Smith agreed to do this, and, noting the desperate straits his visitors were in, he gave them a portion of his private stock of flour and bacon.

The round trip to Beechey took five days and, because the other trading post was also quite low in goods, Smith could only purchase a token amount of oats, flour, sugar and coffee. The Beechey Point trader had no footwear to sell.

On the very night Bahr journeyed to the trading post at Foggy Island, a late storm blew in on the unsuspecting reindeer camp. Gale-driven snow slammed into the herd and caught the men on duty by surprise. In face of the summer blizzard, they could do nothing but retreat to camp. The fierce winds and blinding snow lashed the deer unmercifully, triggering a stampede in which one thousand deer — perhaps one-third of the entire herd — bolted up their back trail and disappeared. It was the worst disaster to strike since the herd had set out almost two years earlier.

As soon as Bahr received word of the incident, he rejoined the men and ordered the Wood brothers and Ivar West to join him in a reconnaissance for the deserters. West flatly refused. He would go nowhere without footwear in proper repair.

Leaving the rest of the crew to watch what remained of the herd, Bahr and the Wood brothers set out after the renegades. The three men spent a week looking for the animals, but when Bahr realized the logistics of the search were all but impossible in the summer, he was forced to postpone it until freeze-up.

To hold the remainder of the herd where they were proved to be a tough task because of desolate grazing grounds. Bahr reported:

> Here along the coast is very poor feed even in summer. No moss and too cold to grow grass or leafs. Low land. Nothing but lakes, swamps,

> full of water . . . I am fright our herd will get sickness such as footrot, the country is too low wet swampy and poor feed.[11]

How could Bahr extricate himself from his mushrooming predicament? He needed mukluks and food, and, if he was going to fire anyone, he would need replacements. In addition, his best men, Tommy and Peter Wood, wanted their families.

The answer to his problems was the trader, Jack Smith, who undertook the job of bailing out the besieged trail boss by doing what he could to help him. Firstly, he garnered enough grub at Beechey Point to last Bahr for two more months. Then he sailed west again, this time going all the way to Barrow. He wired Alfred Lomen that the Wood brothers were desperate enough to pay six hundred dollars of their own money to have their families flown to the Saganavirktok River. The trader also advised that he was willing to hire herders for Bahr at Barrow and assured Lomen they would be experienced. Of all the items Smith mentioned in his telegram to Alfred, one buried at the end of the message was overlooked, or if not, was simply ignored. It read: "Bahr started back over the trail . . . to pick up strays which believed many."[12]

Alfred's return wire made no comment on Bahr's sally. Smith was informed that the families of the Wood brothers had been contacted and would leave Nome aboard the trading ship *Patterson* on August 8. He was also authorized to hire the men as mentioned. Lomen advised Smith to inform Bahr that all boats headed his way had been requested to assist him.

J. W. Smith lent a valuable hand in restoring equilibrium to the operation. He obtained twenty-five pairs of boots and had all of the mukluks resewn and repaired. In addition, he kept Lomen informed as to what was going on. He explained in another wire that the herd would have very little trouble on the long stretch between the "Sag" and Shingle Point, three hundred miles to the east, as there was plenty of high ground immediately back of the coast with copious forage.

The trader completed the transactions at Barrow and sailed back to his Saganavirktok trading post, having hired on Bahr's behalf Mark Noksana and Moses Konuk of Barrow, Terrence Driggs from Point Hope, Albert Peluk of Kobuk, and Clare Panerook from the Foggy Island area. Bahr laid off four men that summer. They were West and Nilluka, and two Eskimos, Theodore Kingeak and Sam Segeok.

The new men were eager to work, but contrary to what Smith had stated in his wire to Lomen, several of the newcomers had little experience, and at first were more of a handicap than an asset.

The *Patterson* arrived with the families of the Wood brothers at the end of September 1931. Their presence immediately upgraded the situation. The wives took on the job of cooking, making a vast improvement over Bahr's efforts. In addition, the women were invaluable when it came to keeping such important items as mukluks in repair. But, at best, trailing a herd was a rugged existence for the women and children even though they were used to life in the Arctic.

Concurrent with the arrival of the Woods' families from the west, the Lapp contingent under the tutelage of Erling Porsild reached the reindeer station in the Mackenzie delta after a lengthy trip from Norway.

Porsild had hired Mikkel Pulk, Mathis Hatta, and Aslak Tornensis at Kautekeino, Norway. Since the botanist was pressed for time when he was in Norway, his options in hiring herders had been limited. He wanted only married men to work the station because he figured they would be less likely to break the contract than single men. This led to an amusing incident. After signing Pulk and Tornensis, Porsild offered the third post to Mathis Hatta. However, Mathis was not married and had no immediate prospects for a wife. Not to be undone by such a requirement and lose his chance at adventure in Canada's northland, Mathis went out one morning and came back that night with a bride. That had to be the whirlwind courtship to end all such courtships.

The Third Year

CHAPTER 9

Backtracking

When the curtain of winter closed down on the Arctic Ocean's shores, the players on that vast barren stage were again cut off from their auditors. During the short, two-month summer, trading ships plied the coast and were instruments for transporting messages. After freeze-up, communication depended on more primitive methods such as dog teams, or just plain "moccasin telegraph" wherein news was transferred verbally from one hunter or trapper to the next and relayed, ripple-like, from one community to another. Since the drive was avoiding the settlements because of reindeer herds located along the coast, it was that much more difficult for Bahr to exchange information with the Lomens.

The July stampede had so thoroughly decimated the herd that by mid-November 1931, when the drive should have been preparing to move east again, the total number of deer, including the additions of the fawn crop, was only eighteen hundred head. By this time, Bahr had driven the shattered flock of ruminants thirty miles east to the Shaviovik River, the mouth of which was half way between the "Sag" on the west and the Canning River. Rut had just ended when Bahr was informed that some of the missing animals had been seen. Passing hunters told him they had spotted five hundred deer with Lomen ear marks between the headwaters of the Kuparuk and the Colville rivers.

Bahr contemplated the idea of going back for them. Since it was impossible to obtain an opinion from the Lomens on such a crucial decision, it weighed heavily on his mind. The main herd was now so reduced in numbers that, if delivered, the Lomens would receive little more than the two partial payments already received rather than the full contracted amount. But if the trail boss wanted to recover the wayfarers, he also knew he would have to take half of the surviving herd back with him, in order to entice the dissidents to join up with them. If he lost those deer too, the drive would be a complete loss.

He had yet another worry: suppose the reindeer reported by the hunters were no longer there. The entire back trip, roughly three hundred miles both ways, would then be a complete waste of time. Reindeer were "homers" and not unlike horses in that they could be expected to drift up their back trail.

However, if diverted by predators or a caribou herd, they would be off in another direction, and it would be impossible for Bahr to locate them.

Bahr pondered the dollar-and-cents aspect of the loss of a thousand deer in the stampede. At the contracted price of sixty-five dollars a head, it amounted to sixty-five thousand dollars, not to mention the proportional waste of energy and provisions used in driving that segment of the herd this far. Bahr hypothesized that if he retrieved half the strays, and was able to hold the line on the deer that remained, his trip would not have been in vain, and he could meet the contracted quota. After weighing all the factors, Bahr reckoned it would be worth the gamble.

Bahr selected Peter Wood to supervise the crew that stayed behind to watch the half of the herd he would leave on the Shaviovik River, and named Tommy Wood, Terrence Driggs, and Edwin Allen to go with him in search of the lost reindeer.

Then, with nine hundred deer in tow, Bahr and his men struck out along the back trail in mid-November. The goal of their search was about one hundred and fifty miles distant. They crossed the Saganavirktok River, where Bahr sent Driggs back with instructions for Peter Wood to move his half of the herd to the "Sag", where there was more feed available, and to wait there until his return.

Bahr's group angled southwest over the wind-swept tundra and traversed the Kuparuk to reach the Colville. The weather became progressively worse as they followed the Colville River upstream toward the mountains. Fierce storms and temperatures that dipped to sixty below zero made it a full-time chore to retain the deer they were already driving, without having to worry about the animals they were searching for. Bahr, Wood, and Allen were forced to make camp in late December to wait out the weather. They put up a tent, which they reinforced with snow blocks so it would not blow away.

After two long weeks, the weather broke, and Bahr sent Allen to Beechey Point with a dog team to get food. Allen was a superior man on the trail and Bahr was confident he would get through.

The young Eskimo had barely left camp when yet another storm roared down from the polar sea and he was forced to hole up.

Meanwhile, Bahr and Wood, though worried about Allen, were preoccupied with keeping themselves alive. They managed to rustle up some sticks and twigs to burn, at the same time scratching out meals from what little food supplies they had left. The men hung on as long as they dared, but after a week Allen still had not shown up. By now they were completely out of food, so Bahr sent Wood to the nearest native camp to borrow whatever he could get and to try and find out what had happened to Allen.

When Wood arrived at the Eskimo camp, Allen was not there, but Tommy was able to obtain some flour and meat which he took back to Bahr. This was sufficient to revitalize the old Lapp, who had taken to lying all day in his sleeping bag to conserve his strength. Wood left him again to search for Allen.

Edwin had been trapped by the storms for two weeks, but eventually made it to Beechey Point. He managed to acquire some food from the trading post there, but on returning was hit by yet another storm. He stacked supplies in the form of an *inuksuk* (man), weighted it down with a loose rock, and left the cache where it could be seen by Wood or Bahr coming down from their camp. Then he, too, sought refuge in the Inuit bivouac.

Tommy Wood discovered the cache, found Allen, and together they returned to camp. The weather improved and the three men rounded up the deer, which had scattered in the storm. Then they set out again, driving the animals farther up the Colville retracing the route they came over just two years before. Then, on a stretch along the river abounding in life-giving lichen, they found four hundred of the vagrants. These animals immediately flocked to the bigger herd, thus presenting Bahr with at least a limited success.

Satisfied that if there were any more deer in the vicinity they would have been with the four hundred, Bahr elected to turn back, and began the countermarch. No sooner had they launched the return journey than abnormally low temperatures enveloped the region in an icy grip. At such times, most animals hole up and wait it out. Wolves, however, who had to have meat to survive, were continually on the prowl. They were attracted to the herd by the fact that the reindeer contingent did not lay-up like caribou. Wolf packs of up to thirty gathered — much higher numbers than the usual family group — in order to bring down game. Their world, like that of any other animal, turned topsy-turvy, especially when prolonged, severe cold clamped down on the countryside.

Some of the wolves that attacked were actually taller than their ungulate victims. Standing up to thirty-eight inches tall at the shoulder and weighing one hundred and eighty pounds, a male wolf was a formidable animal. Front footprints of the predator have been measured at over six inches. This variety, the Gray Wolf, or as it is more commonly known, the "Timber Wolf", is the largest of its species in North America. He may vary in colour from completely white to black. Wolves mate in late winter, with five to fourteen cubs being born in the spring, the number dependent on the fortunes of the group.

Bahr's herd began to attract these predators on a grand scale. The wolves usually waited for a storm, then attacked, cutting out the fawns, the old, and the sick, and even the healthy animals if they could reach them. At this time of year all the bulls had lost their antlers, making even them more vulnerable to the wolves.

The long winter's night made it difficult for Bahr and his companions to spot the marauders. The predators' raids scattered the deer and caused frequent delays because the animals had to be rounded up. For every mile Bahr attempted to push the herd forward, he found himself, at times, going two back. The devastating raiders were more than just a nuisance; they were a serious threat to the recovery operation. Bahr, Wood, and Allen stuck to their jobs, yet could make not much better time than the herd had when it originally covered the route. Only on March 5, 1932, did the exhausted herders finally reach the lower Kuparuk.

Peter Wood, his son Wesley, Moses Konuk, Albert Peluk and Mark Noksana had been left behind to take care of the main herd. The men found a coal seam on the Shaviovik and set up their camp in that area because of the accessibility of the fuel. This was as important as food itself in sustaining life at low temperatures. Despite the coal which they hacked and pried out of the river bank, Peter's group was destined to a niggardly existence that winter. They lived in a house built of blocks of snow with gable ends like a cabin and a canvas stretched over the top, waiting, while a merciless winter sky brooded over them.

The bitter conditions were sharply illustrated when Konuk disappeared in a storm. His associates dared not venture forth to look for their comrade for fear of becoming lost themselves in the swirling snow. When the wind finally died down, Moses staggered into camp more dead than alive, a veritable snow man with a mask of ice crystals clinging to his face.

Terrence Driggs had brought the instructions from Bahr to move the herd west to the Saganavirktok, which Wood handily accomplished. Here, Peter and his family, as well as his brother's wife and children, and the rest of the crew, pitched camp on Franklin's Bluff, a ridge above the valley of the river. Peter, like Bahr, was not without his share of troubles. The crew ran short of food and for the second year in a row, the herders had to send someone north to Smith's trading post at the mouth of the Saganavirktok in hopes of obtaining supplies. Driggs set out downriver, bucking fierce winds. The distance was only twenty miles, but the stiff polar blast at minus forty degrees made the trip seem like an eternity. Finally, half frozen, he struggled into the post, to find that Smith's shelves were bare. Driggs was able to get some tea, but flour, one of the items he needed most, he could not obtain, and he returned to camp without it.

Farther east, at the mouth of the Canning River opposite Flaxman Island, there was another trading post. Peter Wood elected to go there himself in an attempt to obtain food. He fought his way through inclement conditions and finally reached the windswept post. Henry Chamberlain, the proprietor, had supplies for sale, but the question arose as to whether Wood could buy them. The storekeeper put the supplies on the counter as requested by the herder, but when Peter offered to pay for them with a personal cheque, Chamberlain, with a glint of incredulity in his eyes, turned him down. Wood did some fast thinking, and equally glib talking, and told the skeptical trader that he would make the draft good with white fox pelts if he wanted it that way. The storekeeper grudgingly parted with the food, though Wood did not get nearly enough for the large aggregation in camp, who went without flour for a month.

In justice to Chamberlain, the trader was only exercising a precautionary attitude prescribed by the elements. Almost everyone that managed to reach the post purchased the maximum amount of supplies he could afford for fear that the cold spell would go on and on. The trader divvied up the goods as evenly as he judged was fair to insure that each customer got a share. Later on, Wood anticipated the funding problem by sending in white fox skins (trapped by his wife and daughter) along with the purchaser. That way he was able to obtain food with no hassle over the method of payment.

While Wood was holding his half of the herd on the Saganavirktok River, and Bahr was engaged in his walkabout along the Colville, the two contracting parties — the Canadian government and the Lomen brothers — were working up a monumental concern as to where the herd was.

As early as October 1931, Finnie had asked Bob

Porsild to mush a dog team westward from the Mackenzie to find the herd. Bob went to Aklavik to outfit himself for the trip. Coincidentally, a party of Eskimos arrived from Herschel Island and told him the deer had been seen two days west of Demarcation Point, near the Yukon–Alaska border, only two hundred miles from the reindeer station at Kittigazuit.

In transmitting this information to Deputy Minister Cory, as well as to Leonard Baldwin in New York, Finnie commented that if the report was correct, the reindeer drive was making good progress. The Lomens' worries were assuaged by this report, and Bob's trip was cancelled.

Their peace of mind was short-lived. In mid-December, Erling Porsild at Aklavik heard from trappers that the deer were nowhere near the boundary, and that Bob's report had been based on false rumours. The question of the herd's location now took on added importance because of the earlier foul-up.

Major D. L. McKeand, assistant director under Finnie, pointed out in a memo that the government had shifted the funds assigned for the final payment from the next fiscal year to the current one. McKeand wrote: "It is very necessary, therefore, that the Porsild brothers lose no time in getting in touch with the herd and facilitate its delivery before the end of the fiscal year . . . what we are most concerned with now is accurate information as to the whereabouts of the herd and the possibility of its reaching its destination before the 31st March, 1932."[1]

Since Bob was preoccupied with his duties at the Reindeer Station, Erling advised Ottawa that he would make the trip instead. He selected one Lapp, Mikkel Pulk, to go with him. While preparing for the journey, Porsild heard that supplies were scarce along the coast. Therefore, in Aklavik, he hired two native teams to carry dog food ahead and stockpile it at Herschel Island, one hundred and fifty miles to the west. Following them, Porsild and Pulk set out in the third week of January 1932 and reached Herschel in thirteen days. The weather was harsh, with the cold persisting at thirty-five below zero and lower for most of the trip. What could have been a delightful journey in fair weather, turned into a battle with the elements. The two men were quite fortunate in reaching Herschel Island when they did (January 30), as a gale blew in from the south-west right after they arrived, and left them storm bound for two weeks.

A significant change had occurred in 1931 when an election turnover spurred the year-end resignations of Finnie and Cory. At the same time, the Northwest Territories and Yukon Branch of the Department of the Interior was effectively abolished. Henceforth, the territories came under the jurisdiction of the Dominion Lands Board.

H. E. Hume, the newly appointed chairman of

the Board, sent a memo to the Deputy Minister of Interior, H. H. Rowatt, in which he voiced dissatisfaction with the fact there were no long-range plans for administration of the herd after it was delivered. He disclaimed any criticism of the Porsilds, yet added that the general situation at Reindeer Station called for a "strong administrative hand."[2]

In another memo to Rowatt, who remained as a hold-over from the previous administration, Hume requested that he take up the idea of hiring a new man to run the reindeer complex once the herd arrived. He suggested Rowatt place the idea before the new Minister of Interior, Thomas S. Murphy. Rowatt replied that Erling Porsild should be given a chance to show what he could do, and Hume let the matter rest.

Porsild and Pulk absorbed some of the history of Herschel Island during their extended stay. Pauline Cove, the harbour at Herschel, had been the mooring place for the United States whaling fleet from 1889 until 1909. The cove was the finest deep-water port on the north coast. After the heyday of the whalers ran its course, the settlement became a trading station for the Hudson's Bay Company, as well as sub-district headquarters for the Royal Canadian Mounted Police. Principal residents at Herschel when Porsild and Pulk arrived were Eskimo trappers and hunters, trading personnel, missionaries, and the police.

Porsild sought information from Herschel dwellers as to where the reindeer herd might be, and the severity of the weather conditions to the west. Several Inuit who had arrived at the island a month earlier said the herd was somewhere immediately to the west of Tealman Island, this being about twelve miles east of the Saganavirktok delta. Pertaining to the conditions, the natives reported very hard times. There was a great scarcity of dog food, and in fact, food of any kind, and most of the traders were either out of supplies or close to it. Erling could not get the two mushers who had hauled their supplies from Aklavik to continue west because of this news.

The storm moderated on February 12. Porsild and Pulk set out with their dog teams heading northwest along the coast. The weight of the provisions, which were supposed to last them for a month, amounted to eight hundred pounds. They were battered by one westerly storm after another, and while on the trail they met natives who told them it was the worst winter they had seen in a generation.

The two men finally reached a native camp on Tealman Island where they learned the Lomen herd was about three days' dog team journey away. Erling hired an Inuit lad who was knowledgeable of the interior, and they headed for the camp which the youth said was on the Saganavirktok River about seventy miles distant.

They reached the reindeer encampment in the

first week of March. Porsild met Peter Wood, who told him about the stampede in July, and explained Bahr's departure in November to recapture the lost deer. Wood added that Bahr had planned to be back by January 15, but had not showed up. He had no idea where the old Lapp was.

The absence of Bahr and half the herd was extremely disappointing to Porsild for two reasons. Firstly, he would not be able to talk with Bahr, and secondly, for the indefinite aspects of the situation that still existed. Porsild was at a loss as to whether the number of deer in Wood's camp was the total that now remained, or not. What would he report to his superiors? He could wait with Wood and his men in hopes Bahr would show up, but if the Lapp was bivouacked somewhere waiting for the weather to improve, he might not come in for weeks. Erling elected to return to the coast where at least there was some circulation of people and news.

No sooner had he reached the Tealman camp than he met an Eskimo who had arrived from the west in his absence. The Inuit (probably Clare Panerook) claimed that he had been working for Andy Bahr and had only recently left his employ. He said the trail boss had succeeded in rounding up part of the strays and was now camped on the Kuparuk, five days travelling time from Tealman. He guessed the size of the reclaimed herd to be at least one thousand deer, including that part of the herd used to lure the mavericks back. That news gave Porsild cause for optimism.

Erling now felt that he could depart, but first he left a message for Bahr. He said that once the herd was reunited, he saw no reason it could not be moved two hundred miles east to Herschel and pastured there for the summer. He suggested that in the fall the herd could cross again to the mainland and be driven to the Mackenzie delta. Once there, the bay could be traversed in November.

Porsild and Pulk returned to Aklavik in half the time it took them going out, mainly because there was less weight to haul, and they were able to pick up a trail that had already been broken. They reached Aklavik near the end of March, 1932. It had been a prodigious journey: the two men had mushed their dogs almost one thousand miles in one of the worst winters in the history of the Arctic.

For Erling Porsild, the trip was one of the hardest and most unpleasant he had made. Indeed, he had suffered so much, he was predestined to object if asked to do it again.

Porsild had at least found out one thing, and this was that the drive would not reach the reindeer station in the spring. The second estimated date of arrival would, it was now certain, also be missed.

Although larger newspapers had headlined the story of Canada's reindeer purchase in 1929, since then the epic adventure had received almost no coverage. When a story did appear, it seldom reached the front pages. The winter of 1931–32 saw the Albert Johnson case — in which the Royal Canadian Mounted Police tracked down and killed a desperado in the northern wilderness — capture the front-page headlines throughout North America; yet the reindeer hegira, the last and most incredible of all such expeditions on the continent, was barely heard of. One of the reasons for this was the general reluctance of the Canadian government itself to bring attention to it at this time. Ottawa was shy when it came to boasting about an expenditure which was in the one-quarter-million dollar bracket, with the reindeer herd cavorting around the wilderness, sometimes being heard from and sometimes not. Dominion Lands Board Chairman Hume scribbled a note to subordinates on news releases about the drive: "Suggest as little publicity as possible . . ."[3] Bahr would continue to play out his role behind an almost impenetrable veil of wintry silence.

CHAPTER 10

A Stranger Arrives

Under optimal conditions, Andy Bahr might have been able to reach Herschel Island by April, but as Erling Porsild himself had experienced, conditions were seldom optimal on the northern plains. On his outward trip from Aklavik, it had taken Erling thirty-three days to travel almost an equivalent distance, and all that he had to worry about was his dog team.

Bahr finally brought his prodigal herd back to reunite it with Peter Wood's bunch on the "Sag", then pushed the deer east to the Shaviovik. He arrived there in early May — back where he had started from the previous July. He had recovered four hundred of the strays, but according to his own words, he did not gain much more than an endless litany of woes, as is reflected in his discouraging words: "We did not make any head ways we loose just as much by starving and died by sickness play out and left on the trail on account of bad feeding storms foggs all year round, too many caribou, woolves."[1]

Was the search worth the effort, when one considers the time expended and the energy and expense involved? Bahr did not think so, though on balance it probably was. If he had been able to retrieve one thousand deer, his gamble would have been a big success. If he had not undertaken the roundup of the strays, he would have needed another calf crop which would have delayed him another year anyway.

As it was, the fawn yield was satisfactory that spring along the Shaviovik, though the weather could have been better. Bahr wrote: "We are eight men including Tomie Woods boy [Wesley]. Weather condition has been bad since I came to this country, very seldom good weather."

Bahr moved eastward again as soon as all of the fawns were dropped. He crossed the Kavik to the Canning River and descended that to the coast. He intended to remain there until autumn, nursing the herd that now numbered approximately twenty-two hundred.

Summer burst on the Canning River bivouac with surprising swiftness. The compensating factor to offset the rain and the insects, the heat, and the hard walking at this time of the year, was the beauty of the tundra with the sprouting of the verdant summer grass. On a clear day this captivating emerald mat stood in sharp contrast to the powder-blue sky, and from a distance looked like a well-groomed park, compassionate to the eye and deceptively tranquil. Even on a rainy day the limitless land and sky often exhibited countless numbers of rainbows — nature's own searchlights — that cast their arches landwards in a profusion of colour.

Though in many ways hostile to humans in its short season of warmth, the tundra was much more receptive to other forms of life, and in welcoming them to its bosom presented the drovers with a lively and radiant sight on which to rest their eyes after the long winter's night.

Ducks, geese, and swans by the thousands came in to build their nests next to innumerable lakes, ponds, eddies, and sloughs of the northern plain in a wild splurge of activity. The cries of the water birds blended into a symphony that was pleasing to the ear after the silence of winter. The presence of the feathered population gave the herders inclined to hunt them a welcome change of diet.

Clusters of flowers that pleased the eye and diffused a refreshing aroma burst forth to splash the land with colour. Each wave of blossoming plants gave way to another phalanx, and yet another, as summer advanced. These strokes of nature's paintbrush added a unique tint to the giant marsh. Purple crocuses, alabaster stars, crimson fireweed, golden buttercups, and bluebells were just a few of the ingredients that supplied nature's pigmentation.

Along with the effusion of plant life came the

bountiful crops of tasty, sweet, fruit-bearing plants such as crowberries, blueberries, cranberries, and raspberries, upon which both the herders and their charges contentedly fed.

There were moments when all of nature was in perfect harmony for the drovers, as if a composer had finally hit the correct chord. Nothing better exemplified this than when the midnight sun lay on the polar rim of the earth and its rays played off the distant spires of the Brooks Range to the south. A man could glory in the roseate glow that emanated from the peaks is if they were afire with burning embers. Like the shimmering aurora, the colours of the range fluctuated continuously, depending on the angle of the sun above the horizon. One moment the lofty battlements would be draped in a purple mantle, and the next gilded with a golden hue. This was the backdrop to the green, treeless foothills that rose up twenty miles from the coast to break the tedious table of the coastal plain.

Life on the tundra in the summer was life in a hurry. Birds had to build their nests and raise their young quickly, before the precious warmth gave way to winter. Predators, grazing animals, fish, and even insects depended on the short period of warmth to rekindle the species. The Arctic's short summer season demanded a degree of intensity that bordered on carelessness on the part of the fauna. In a way, this favoured the man who took an interest in viewing the antics of wild folk. Whether it was a grizzly swimming a river, or a fox that waited to snatch a ptarmigan, or, high above, a hawk that circled in its perpetual quest for rodents, there were endless life and death scenes being reenacted. The fauna were so preoccupied with their own regeneration they were unfearing of a human bystander who revelled in what he saw.

Edwin Allen must have been such a man. In the journals and correspondence about the drive very little was written about Allen except a few references to the fact that he was there, and had been from almost the beginning. Inclement weather, tortuous obstacles, envy, hostility, and jealous disputes belaboured the drive, yet through it all, Edwin Allen loomed in the background as that sort of unsung individual who was as solid mentally as he was physically. A well-built man, Allen commanded respect in a stalwart, silent way. He was an individual that seemed to fit the picture like no other. Many of the Eskimos grew tired of the monotony and went home. The Lapps, West and Nilluka, were critical of Bahr and left. Some men, like Nakkala, were forced to leave the herd because of illness. Yet always Allen was on hand to take a job that other men gave up. He was to the drive what vertebrae are to an animal: he helped hold it together. His presence was so quiet, it made one wonder if there really was an Edwin Allen, but there was, and he was one of the best.

Because feeding conditions along the coast were not up to his original estimates, Bahr shifted the herd farther up the Canning. Here, housekeeping details kept the men busy. Brush corrals were built and one hundred fawns were castrated. The crew was now comprised wholly of Eskimos with the exception of Bahr. They got along all right and worked well together. Bahr named Peter Wood chief herder of the crew.

Peter Wood, anticipating the birth of a child, moved his wife and family down to the mouth of the Canning and camped near Chamberlain's trading post. The new addition arrived at the lower camp on the Canning in June when a baby girl, Helen, was born to Peter and his wife. A month later, when supplies were expected to arrive, Bahr also moved down from the camp far up the Canning to the coast, leaving herders to watch after the reindeer. In mid-July Captain Pedersen arrived aboard his trading ship and unloaded badly needed supplies, some of which were relayed to the upper camp by the herders leading pack deer.

Summer was waning when Andrew Bahr was struck down by a severe case of ptomaine poisoning after he ate a rancid orange and possibly tainted meat. Peter Wood recalled:

"His stomach got big and swollen, and for two hours he was very bad. We got a hot-water bag for him, which was all we could do. He told us if he died we were to send messages to Lomen Company and tell them what we were going to do."[2]

Still weak in September, Bahr was surprised one day by the arrival of a white man who asked him for a job. The man was David Irwin, a sandy-haired youth of twenty-two years. Irwin's recollections, published later, afforded one of the few outsider's views of the drive.[3]

Young Irwin, originally from the American midwest, was no stranger in Alaska Territory. Before moving to the north coast, he had spent two years in the wilderness region of the Yukon River, south of the Brooks Range. In Nome, he prevailed on Ira Rank, an escapee from Russia after the Czar was overthrown, to give him passage eastwards on Rank's little vessel, the *Trader*. He explained to Rank that he hoped to work for Bahr, whom he knew was leading the drive somewhere out on the tundra.

Rank, a veteran of the Arctic, spotted a certain earnestness about the youth that appealed to him. He agreed to take Irwin as far east along the coast of the Arctic Ocean as conditions would permit, though he stressed to the young adventurer that much depended on the whimsies of the ice pack. Weather conditions were good and the trader let Irwin off at the mouth of the Canning River at the end of August. Irwin walked into Bahr's camp only to encounter seven big Malemutes who snarled their objections to his sudden appearance. He circled around the area where they were chained to stakes only to meet two more dogs, but these were of a better nature. They were sheep dogs who sought a friendly pat. An Eskimo woman, whom Irwin noted wore a light parka and a calico skirt, glanced his way, then took him to Bahr's tent.

Irwin's first view of Bahr was of a gaunt old man lying on a pile of deer hides that covered a mat made out of willows. Bahr's eyes opened wide with surprise at seeing the youth; then he gestured for the visitor to sit down on a wooden crate.

Bahr was starved for news, and asked Irwin to describe what was going on in the world. He was particularly interested in the stock market crash of which he had heard generalities but no details. Irwin described plunging prices and nation-wide unemployment that had been caused by the economic disaster. On hearing this, the old Lapp expressed the opinion he was lucky to be with the trail drive.

The young adventurer was invited to a dinner comprising bannock and steaming caribou steaks. While enjoying the meal, Irwin hit a sympathetic note with the older man when he explained his reason for coming to the Arctic coast. He told Bahr he was heading east to look for clues to the fate of Sir John Franklin and his crew of one hundred and twenty-nine men who had disappeared in the vicinity of the Boothia Peninsula, far to the east, north of Hudson Bay, with two ships, the *Erebus* and *Terror*, in 1848.

Andy Bahr registered interest in Irwin's search. He stated that he knew Knud Rasmussen, the polar explorer, who also was fascinated by the riddle of Franklin's disappearance. He advised Irwin to search for clues on the east side of King William's Island, instead of the west side, as many previous expeditions had attempted. "That's where I should look, Dave," Bahr said, "if I were going up there."[4]

Irwin needed funds to help him along with his adventure and consequently sought a job with the herd. He added that he would not be staying on for the entire drive because of his obsession with the Franklin mystery; he planned to travel farther eastward that winter. Bahr thought over Irwin's request for a job, then agreed to hire Irwin for a probationary period of two weeks, if the Eskimo herders agreed to it.

The two men talked the night away. Then, after sleeping through most of the day and into the next night, Irwin was awakened and introduced by Bahr to Edwin Allen, who was in his twenties and about the same age as Irwin. Allen was getting ready to leave for the upper camp, and was designated by Bahr to instruct the newcomer in the art of herding reindeer. Irwin helped the Eskimo in assembling food for their trip. Since they would be carrying the supplies on their backs, and would be gone for at least two weeks, it was simple fare. They took along tea, flour, baking powder, and jerked caribou meat. They planned to add to this diet by netting fish and shooting caribou if they got the chance.

Irwin was assigned a herd dog by Allen. He called the small black and white border collie "Chappy", who though small, was an experienced herd dog as was "Kobuk", Edwin Allen's own dog. The canines were rigged up with packs and toted their own food.

The two men set out from the main camp the next day. Morning fog obliterated the sun above the mist, but the heat was still oppressive. They hiked for six hours. Irwin by this time was soaked with sweat, yet his feet were numb from being immersed in the frigid water that oozed up from the sponge-like moss over which they struggled. They adjusted their clothing and walked for another six hours before Allen decided to make camp at a dry spot on the tundra.

The next morning they reached Peter Wood's camp and unloaded their heavy packs, some of the contents of which were slated for the men of the out-camp. Peter explained that the deer were scattered over the foothills of the Brooks Range a few miles to the south. Four herders were out on the range rounding them up. Irwin and Allen's job was to bring in a band of deer that grazed near a creek several miles away. Once these were driven to the vicinity of Peter's camp, and the other deer were brought in, the entire herd was to be held in the immediate vicinity until frost rid the country of insects. Then the deer were to be pushed to Bahr's camp and the reindeer drive would resume its eastward journey.

Allen and Irwin set out again after lightening their packs. In a short time, they had reached the creek, forded it, and spotted the deer mentioned by Wood. They were both surprised to see the band was a much larger group than they had been led to believe. The deer, with their excellent sense of smell, had become conscious of the steady approach of Allen and Irwin; they were visibly spooked when they saw the men, and went into a mill.

Irwin, seeing this spectacle for the first time, gazed at the herd in wonder. The open hills afforded him a panoramic view and he was briefly mesmerized by the unfolding scene. The two dogs immediately swung wide in opposite directions around the herd without so much as a sound or a hand gesture on the part of Allen. Irwin was amazed at their quickness and capabilities with respect to figuring out the actions of the deer. Even more surprising were Edwin's shouted instructions to run full-tilt away from the deer. He followed Allen away from the herd and dropped to the ground.

Allen noticed the perplexed look on Irwin's face and explained the unusual behaviour of the semi-wild deer. They were extremely timid and tended to panic when strange scents came their way. By running away, the men allowed them to calm down.

They again approached the herd, with Allen in the lead. When the deer threatened to stampede, Allen, Irwin, and the dogs would retreat. This tactic was repeated over and over again until the deer became accustomed to their presence. Once the deer were relatively stable, the two men and dogs continuously circled around the herd, gradually tightening the diameter of the circle. Each time the reindeer became visibly excited, the men would slack off. Gradually they brought the deer closer together until they were tame enough to let the dogs watch over them.

David and Edwin remained three weeks with the band as they slowly guided the deer toward Peter Wood's field camp. The dogs circled the deer constantly while the men put pressure on the herd in the direction they wanted it to go. They finally reached the field camp at the end of September, and turned the reindeer loose with the animals brought in by the other herders.

Irwin was particularly impressed by the conduct of the shepherd dogs. The dogs worked so hard that they wore themselves out as much as the men. He noted that the dogs were bred for the job and their sense of responsibility was keen, even to the point of over-tending the deer. Occasionally, at night they would become overly conscientious and hold the animals in too compact a group. Then the men would have to call them off as otherwise the deer would panic, and stampede.

Peter Wood struck the out-camp in October and the deer were driven downriver to Bahr's main camp. The mosquitoes were now gone and life was easier on both animals and men. Rutting continued throughout autumn and since the female deer were well rested and in good condition, they accepted the bulls which meant there would be a good fawn crop the next spring.

Allen and Irwin got along well. Bahr had given Irwin an Eskimo dictionary, which he used often in attempting to learn Eskimo words. He practiced them on Allen, who was of much help to him. Bahr seemed satisfied with Irwin's work and hired the newcomer at fifty dollars a month.

Shortly afterwards, snow fell and stayed. Sleds that had been toted to camp by boat from their point of abandonment the previous spring were loaded with supplies and gear. Some sleds were so heavily loaded that as many as five deer were hooked up single file to haul them in a train. Irwin's job was to mush the dog team that consisted of the seven ponderous brutes he had met when he first arrived at the main camp. The dogs were quite capable of pulling a one-thousand-pound load, though they were slightly out of condition because they had been tied up all summer.

In his memoir Irwin paid respect to Bahr's efficient handling of the huge amount of detail needed to successfully move the drive's entourage. He recalled:

> Gathering . . . reindeer together in a huge, churning band, distributing his men so that the deer would be kept moving with a minimum of danger from fright and stampede, following a course that offered both good feeding and conditions favorable for transportation, remembering every detail necessary to the existence of those under his leadership as well as the safety of his animal charges — these were some of the things that

Bahr was responsible for . . . [5]

Bahr strapped on skis and led the herd on its eastern swing. The shepherd dogs moved up to cover the flanks of the herd as it moved out. Three herders, each leading a deer that hauled a sled, trailed along the sides of the mass exodus. Irwin brought up the rear with the sled dogs.

The herd could only be moved a few miles a day at first, due to the fact the deer, particularly the young, were not used to being confined, and were unruly. Gradually, however, the ritual of life on the trail became second nature for them and the herd resumed its normal rhythms.

Wolves moved in from the nearby mountains and proved to be a perpetual threat, requiring unending vigilance. Irwin found life on the trail to consist of days and weeks of monotonous, dreary work through long hours and intense cold. There was no escaping the heavy responsibility of watching the deer. The pressure to keep the herd together was always uppermost in their minds. Day and night, the never-ending fear of a stampede plagued the men. Adequate forage was a prerequisite to preventing stampedes; thus it was important that Bahr and his men find a route where lichen grew in abundance.

Irwin drove the dog team and also helped mind the herd. The cold grew more intense as winter came on; the Arctic nights lengthened. Irwin spent long hours alone, guarding one side of the herd, often huddled up in his sleeping bag on the cold snow. Chappy would join him at such times. The pleasant little mutt was always ready and willing to race after deer that strayed away.

Fires became a luxury when the herd ventured into the woodless areas between river valleys. Firewood was packed along with the herders, but there was never enough. Without a fire, there were no hot meals, and Irwin, like the others, occasionally ate raw caribou or raw whitefish or even *muk-tuk* (raw whale skin and blubber).

As the herd became more accustomed to travel after a long summer of idle grazing on the tundra, the deer's pace quickened, adding pressure to Irwin's duties. Stop-overs to rest the reindeer were less frequent as Bahr did his best to make good time during one of the few parts of the year when the deer could be driven without being inhibited by fawning, swamps, or rutting season.

Increasing numbers of deer began to bolt from the herd, due to the hastened tempo of the drive. This meant that Irwin and the other herders were forced to double or triple the distance covered, tracking strays and bringing them back to the main herd. Sleep became all but impossible, and hunger was a constant agony. David held up well under the adverse conditions, and more than ever admired the physical and mental strength of the men he worked with, particularly Andrew Bahr, who may have been bent, but was never broken, by the difficulties.

Eventually, when the expedition was down to only a little tea, almost no tobacco, a sprinkling of flour, some dried meat, and a steady diet of raw fish, Irwin told Bahr he was going to leave. The trail boss gave him a cheque for his work, and wished him good luck. Irwin trekked to nearby Barter Island, where he was made welcome by Tom Gordon who supplied him with food and a dog team to continue his long journey.

The Fourth Year

CHAPTER 11

Stampede

Everything appeared to be going right for Bahr in late autumn, 1932. The deer were well rested, the does had been bred, the crew seemed to be amiable, and with the exception of the limited supply of "white man's" food, the drive was in the best condition it had been since the summer on the Kobuk River.

Expectations for the arrival of the herd were optimistic on the Canadian side of the line. Through the fall the Lapp families pitched in to put up additional fencing. A summer corral was built six miles down the Mackenzie River from the reindeer station. The main camp was expanded to include not only cabins for the Lapps, but also for Peter and Tommy Wood and their families, as the brothers had agreed to take on the job of working with the Canadians for at least two years.

Ironically, at just this time the administrators of the drive — Leonard Baldwin and the Lomens — reached a peak in their worries over the progress of the herd. Bahr was not the most articulate of writers; much work was needed in reading his messages. Even the Lomens, who were adept at fathoming what was going on in the old man's mind, were hard put to comprehend their foreman's plans. Someone was needed to tabulate his performance and to relate the drive's progress.

To compound the poor communications, what news there was from the drive seemed to be tainted by a litany of criticism drifting into the Lomen offices from the men Bahr had fired the preceding summer. They had now reached Nome and Kotzebue and presented their side of the argument — a refrain definitely not in Bahr's favour. The trail boss could offer no defence against these diatribes because he was still in the field. This disparagement served to exacerbate the worries of the administrators, and was reflected in a letter that Baldwin wrote to Hume on October 17 in which he sought assistance for Bahr's crew in the field to prevent "the straying of the herd and in warding off the attack of wolves."[1]

Baldwin, with a reputation to protect, suggested that Erling Porsild and the Canadian Lapps join up with Bahr to make doubly certain the herd was delivered to its destination the following spring, 1933. He emphasized the fact that Porsild should join the herd for his knowledge of the area and to reassure Bahr as to what was ahead of him. He wrote: "Mr. Porsild has been over the territory to be traversed at least three times and has made a report on the feeding conditions." Baldwin was of the opinion that "Andrew [Bahr] is imagining not only real difficulties that do exist but many that do not."

This letter was to touch off the biggest dispute of the drive, at the centre of which was Erling Porsild.

Hume, under whose jurisdiction the reindeer contract was now administered, had no objections to Baldwin's requests and, in a note delineating Baldwin's points, instructed Erling Porsild to shift his three Lapps westward to help Bahr. Hume added: "The government representatives [i.e. Porsild] will be subject to the orders of the superintendent of the drive."[2]

The fact that the request did not go over very well with Porsild was evident in his reply. He lambasted the chairman for entertaining the idea of employing the Lapps and himself on the trail. And he injected a few caustic remarks that bordered on prejudice in his bitterness over being committed as a herder under the supervision of Bahr.

Porsild informed Hume that the three Lapps would not go. The terms of their contract stated they were to act as reindeer herders at the station, and there were no provisions to undertake extensive journeys to Alaska. He said a prolonged trip at that time of the year involved great personal risk and would separate the Lapps from their families for an indefinite period. The incensed botanist took the opportunity to point out that Mikkel Pulk, who had accompanied him on his herculean journey of the winter before, had received no extra allowance for his effort.

The irate Dane stated he was still suffering from rheumatism and digestive complications which resulted from that trip. He complained that after six years with the department he now received less consideration and remuneration than when he had been first employed. One last straw as far as Porsild was concerned was his apparent appointment as a herder: "I have never undertaken to herd reindeer personally," he seethed, "and I do not intend to."

Erling Porsild's temper hit the boiling point with respect to serving under Bahr: "Your instruction to place myself under the direction and subject to instructions of the Lapp, Andrew Bahr, I can only consider a personal insult." Porsild concluded the wire by saying he would quit if the instructions were allowed to stand.[3]

Communications by wire and letter were difficult at the best of times. Innuendos could be read in that had not been intended the way they seemed. Erling Porsild may have overreacted to the telegram, but then, he had been six years on the project, ruining his health in the process, and was like a bomb waiting for a charge to set it off. The telegram had done just that.

Erling's bitter reply was forwarded to Rowatt, the Deputy Minister of the Interior, who poured oil on the troubled waters: "There is no desire or intention of asking Mr. Porsild to act as a reindeer herder, but he is asked to assist Andrew Bahr with advice because he and his brother are the only persons who know the country through which the herd is to travel."[4]

Meantime, Leonard Baldwin in New York divined that the crux of the problem was money. He offered twenty-five hundred dollars extra to Porsild and the three Lapps if they would assist Bahr and his men until June 1, 1933, or until the drive was completed, whichever came first. This proposal was relayed to the reindeer station and the contentious point was resolved when Erling Porsild tentatively accepted the offer. He assigned his brother to the task of leading the Lapps to Bahr, and divvied up the allocated funds so that Bob Porsild received one thousand dollars and the Lapps, five hundred dollars each. Erling, because of health problems, would remain at the reindeer station, replacing Bob as head of the construction program there.

Erling Porsild drew up a contingency contract pertaining to the unscheduled venture, which the three Lapps signed. Firstly, they vowed to remain in the field for the prescribed length of the contract. Secondly, they consented to work under Bahr's orders; and thirdly, they agreed to forfeit all claims to extra compensation if they left before fulfilling the terms of the contract. On November 22, 1932, Bob Porsild, Mikkel Pulk, Mathis Hatta, and Aslak Tornensis left the delta for Bahr's encampment. The drive at this point certainly looked like it was near termination. Bahr had commenced moving eastward in November with a good crew of eight men, including himself, and four reinforcements who were on the way. This would bring the crew to its largest complement since the drive began.

The Canadian delegation had a good run west and met up with the herd at Icy Reef on December 4 after a two-hundred-mile trip by dog team and skis. The men travelled on land for most of the trip, rather than the easier route by sea ice, in order to check out the feed, which the Lapps estimated to be adequate for the herd.

Porsild's arrival was not only a surprise to Bahr, but also tantamount to giving another dollar to a man who already had a million. Bahr's statement put Bob Porsild in a dilemma. He explained his instructions to the Lapp, realizing Bahr did not know of the hullabaloo on the "outside" that had led up to his arrival. Bahr heard him out and then acceded to Porsild and his men staying.

The situation with regards to the trail drive now took on the characteristics of a syllogism gone askew. The previous July, Bahr had requested more men to help him handle the drive. Alfred Lomen had referred this need to Baldwin, who prevailed on Hume, who told Erling Porsild, who sent Bob Porsild and three Lapps, who finally arrived six months after the request. Yet the arrival of the "help" would have the unintended effect of almost ruining the operation. One reason had to do with the subtle psychology of men engaged in such a solitary expedition. Though they may gripe, and be lonely, the intrusion of new personalities may upset the unspoken, delicate balance among the crew members. Second, rations were already at rock bottom, without having four more mouths to feed. Porsild brought supplies along, but not enough to keep his group in food forever. This situation was to initiate a grinding dispute that all but destroyed the drive because of ill feelings and rancour on the part of the newly arrived Lapps. They did not get enough food from the trail boss.

Bob Porsild's presence, however, offered one advantage: he provided more intelligible source of communications between Bahr and the administrators in Ottawa, New York, Seattle, and Nome.

Andrew Bahr and his expanded outfit drove the reindeer east from Icy Reef to reach Herschel Island on schedule. Here, he ran into trouble over goods that were supposed to have been dropped off there by trader C. T. Pedersen.

Captain Pedersen was a legendary figure in the Arctic. For thirty years, his Northern Whaling and Trading Company had served small communities scattered along the expanse of the Arctic coast, from Alaska on the west, right across to Ellesmere Island in the eastern Canadian Arctic. In order to better serve far-flung customers, his company placed offices in New York City, and in Oakland, California. Of all the trading ventures that have ever existed in the north, it is doubtful if any were more consistently exposed to greater hazards than that of Pedersen in his little supply schooner, the *Patterson*. Year after year, he plied the ice-clogged shores of the Arctic, as dependable to his customers as the neighbourhood newspaper boy or mailman. His orders for equipment and supplies were received up to a year ahead of time, and often letters posted one year did not reach him until the next.

Pedersen had dropped off supplies during the summer to be held in bond for Bahr at Herschel Island. He left instructions with the police corporal stationed there to release the goods when Bahr arrived. The corporal, however, had moved to Aklavik for the winter and apparently failed to advise his replacement of the directive. Thus the trail boss was turned down when he asked for the shipment.

Frustrated by this turn of events, Bahr solicited the Hudson's Bay Company post at Herschel for what stores they had available, but did not get much. This foul-up was to be a harbinger of more difficulties.

The pilgrims moved out again. The weather held good until the herd reached the vicinity of Kay Point, forty miles east of Herschel Island, near the end of January 1933. The expedition was hit by a series of blizzards that raked the coast with howling winds and blinding snow. Again the reindeer were in jeopardy because under those conditions the menace of wolves was at its greatest. Mathis Hatta described the situation:

> We would have to be out watching the herd, walking around them, night and day looking for wolves and chasing some of the deer that would stray and get lost.
>
> It was sixty below — sometimes seventy — and cold winds. We would work in shifts of twenty-four hours, but sometimes we would have to keep working for forty-eight hours or more. We didn't get much sleep anytime.[5]

The fact that Hatta constantly returned to the subject of wolves in his recollections emphasized how serious a menace the predators were. He continued:

> We were always looking for wolves. They wouldn't come very close in when it was light, but they would come around in the dark and when it was stormy. You couldn't see them. You would just fire in the air and scare them away. But they got quite a few reindeer just the same.
>
> They were mostly white wolves like the snow, but some were brown. There were sometimes twenty in a bunch.

The bad weather meant the drive hardly moved, but this did not mean the herders had it any easier.

> We would move the herd about a mile a day. They would scrape the snow away with their front feet to eat the moss. We had to keep watch, walking around them — sometimes run like reindeer . . . it wasn't so bad while the deer kept close together in one bunch, but when some of them strayed we had to go after them.

The storms persisted as the expedition crept eastward, and as the reindeer moved farther on, the British and Richardson mountain ranges closed in on the coast. These bastions furnished a refuge for even larger packs of wolves that carried out their incessant raids against the deer.

The onslaught of wind and snow persisted through the entire month of February, battering men, dogs, and deer with unremitting ferocity. The drovers knew they were engaged in a race against time because the fawning period was expected in the second week of April. Each day, the does grew heavier and it became more difficult for them to travel. If the herd did not reach the Mackenzie crossing point quickly enough, the trek over the ice could not be undertaken at all because of the awkwardness of the females and the lack of food to sustain them on the twenty-mile open stretch of Mackenzie Bay.

Bahr and his men reached Shingle Point on March 1, 1933. The herd had travelled one hundred and fifty miles in four months, averaging little better than a mile a day. This was good time, considering the adversity of the elements.

Shingle Point harboured an Anglican mission school for Eskimo youths. The school was run by the chief of the mission, who was assisted by a small staff of three teachers from England. Forty students of both sexes attended the school and were taught English and fundamental grade school subjects.

A week after arriving at the mission, Andrew Bahr found time to dispatch a letter to Ralph Lomen in Seattle. The tone of the note was optimistic. He seemed to be satisfied that the deer would recuperate from the depleting effects of the last four months on the trail. In his colourful vernacular, he wrote:

> Just a few lines to let you know that we are here now at Shingle Point. We had hard times to get here on account of the continuous storms, short, short days and bad feeding conditions. No moss only here and there spot. Our herd gotten very week, quite a few deer gotten lost, killed by wolves and dead on the road. We been here now for one week, here is good feed, moss and the snow condition is good also the weather has been good since we came here. We are soon going to move again thirty miles more south easterly direction close to the crossing place. The crossing will be the first week of April. Mr. Porsild and myself we are going after a couple of days to

examine the crossing place. We will go as far
as their station.[6]

A dialogue now commenced between Bahr and Bob Porsild over when the herd should be delivered. Bob was anxious to drive the deer across the bay ice as quickly as possible. Every day of delay meant the pregnant does would find it that much more difficult to reach Ellice Island, the first of several that squatted like so many stepping stones across the bay, until the reindeer station was reached. Porsild judged that these islands were at least sufficient in moss to entice the herd forward as it was pushed through the delta to its destination. The distance from Ellice Island to the reindeer station was about sixty miles.

Bahr wanted to do just the opposite. Obviously, economic considerations influenced their two lines of reasoning to a certain degree. If the animals were delivered immediately, as Porsild wanted, the fawns would be dropped at the station, and the Canadian government would gain up to one thousand calves free of charge. Of even more importance to Porsild was the fact that their birth on the east side of the Mackenzie would centre their homing instinct where it should be.

On the other hand, if Bahr held the animals and managed to increase the size of the herd, the Lomens would receive more money than if the crossing was made before fawning. The problem with holding the deer was that the young animals would not be capable of making such a journey without at least a month to gain strength. However, by that time the bay ice would be impossible to cross because it would be rotten, and the herd would have to skulk in the field until the next winter.

Porsild was persistent in his argument, and Bahr eventually gave in to his reasoning. They went to the mouth of the Blow River, aptly named for the monumental gales that frequently swept the area, to survey the crossing point. It looked satisfactory to them and they returned to Shingle Point.

The words "beware the ides of March" could have been offered to Porsild and Bahr as a warning worth heeding. March 16 brought down a storm so fierce that it rivalled in intensity any blow that had ever hit the Shingle Point region. The vicious winds ripped roofs off some of the buildings spread along the coast, already built low and shaped to withstand Arctic winds. Snow piled up in deep drifts on the lee side of every standing object. These crystals took on the velocity of buckshot due to the wind. Neither man nor deer could face such pellets. The men could not keep their faces into the wind under this barrage and turned from it. Even the reindeer, contrary to their usual habit, drifted with the tempest.

Bahr and Porsild realized that holding the herd was all but impossible with visibility at less than a foot, but the attempt had to be made. The drovers rushed into the night accompanied by their shepherd dogs. The latter knew by scent where the deer were and raced to contain them, darting this way and that to stop the sallies of those deer that made a run for it. Despite the severity of the storm, the shepherd dogs might have held the reindeer if it were not for the inevitable appearance of wolves, whose distant howls summoning the pack carried forth on the wind like the mournful wails of banshees forecasting the imminence of death. Under cover of snow and darkness, the inexhaustible marauders of the northern plains infiltrated the herd, and flushed it like a covey of ptarmigan. There was little the valiant herd dogs could do in the face of such attacks. Fortunately for them, the wolves were bent on bigger game or the dogs, too, would have fallen victim to the carnivores' powerful jaws.

The herders fired their guns into the air in order to fend off the wolves, but to try and hit one was impossible. Even scare tactics failed as the rifles' reports were lost in the howling wind.

When the storm finally subsided the drovers set about the difficult, painstaking job of rounding up the deer. This meant donning skis and launching themselves in the direction in which the deer were last seen. The extent and length of the storm often determined how far the animals had travelled. Wolf attacks fragmented and dispersed the deer even more. If sled deer were held during the storm, they, too, would be enlisted for the roundup. They could be counted on to scent the others while at the same time pulling a searcher on a sled.

One important chore was to find the nucleus of the herd. No matter how violent the storm, there was usually at least one group substantially larger than the rest, and to that group the other deer would be attracted when driven near it. The job of rounding up a stampeded herd was always difficult because it strained all the resources of the drive to the utmost. The entire complement of men would have to be used because of the time factor involved — the longer the deer were left unattended, the more fractious and difficult they were to control when they finally were found. Thus, at times the herder might go three or four days with virtually no sleep, grabbing food on the run, cooking over little primus stoves they packed with them to warm up beans frozen in cakes carried in the pockets of their parkas.

This debacle was one of those occasions. It took more than a week to round up the herd, and the results of their labour indicated a ruinous setback. Many of the does, heavy with fawns, either died from exhaustion while struggling through the blizzard, or were killed by wolves. The final count, when it was all over, showed that three hundred deer had been lost. This reverse showed how vulnerable a trail drive of deer could be — and would remain until final delivery and counting of the animals at the corrals on the east side of the Mackenzie delta.

After surveying the remnants of the herd, Bob Porsild and Bahr were both in agreement that it would be futile to go ahead with an attempt to cross Mackenzie Bay. Bob hired a dog team to take him the seventy-five miles to Aklavik, where he filed a report with the Canadian government and wrote the Lomen brothers of the loss. Coming from Porsild, this message presented a more explicit conception of the tremendous toll exacted by the elements, and served to partially exonerate Bahr in the face of criticism that he was deliberately delaying the drive:

> In my opinion, no effort has been spared since we connected with the herd in December to effect delivery this spring. Extremely contrary weather condition have prevailed and only by luck have four human lives not been lost while attempting to regain control of deer during blizzards and wolf attacks. Herd still numbers about two thousand head.[7]

Porsild went on to the reindeer station after filing his report, as there would be no need for his services at the herd. The deer would now have to be held through the fawning season, then grazed on the west side of the delta through the summer and fall. Porsild judged a crossing could be attempted in November 1933.

Bahr took a welcome "leave of absence" from the herd by accompanying Porsild to the reindeer station, where he conferred briefly with Erling before returning to the herd.

CHAPTER 12

Too Long on the Trail

Leonard Baldwin, after a sudden illness, died at Methodist Episcopal Hospital in Brooklyn, New York on January 25, 1933. He was sixty-six. His death was not only a great personal loss to the Lomens, but removed an individual who was of prime importance to their operations, both as vice-president and financial supporter.

Leonard had taken on the task of principal correspondent and negotiator with the Canadian government in respect to the reindeer drive. The parties to the contract had been brought together through his offices, and being somewhat of a risk-taker in his own right, Leonard had worked hard to make the venture a success. His interest in people was an integral part of his lifestyle. In underwriting the Lomen brothers in their Alaskan ventures, he had been aware that he was also helping the

Eskimos of the region. His empathy for the disadvantaged was exemplified by his other philanthropical gestures. He served for twenty-five years as president of the Young Men's Christian Association in Orange County, New Jersey, and as Chairman of the Welfare Federation in that county for two years. He was a modest man who avoided the limelight. An example of this was an "oration" he gave at Drew University (originally founded as a religious institution) to which he had donated a building. The speech lasted ninety seconds: "It would," he said, "aid Drew to send forth better men, better preachers, better doers of his word."[1]

Arthur Baldwin stepped into the breach to fulfill his brother's commitments with respect to the reindeer operations, taking his place working with Carl Lomen and the Canadians. Arthur was known for his cheerful disposition, though he was not insensitive to the seriousness of financial setbacks. An example of Arthur's outlook was a jingle he wrote and sent to an executive of a freight company that was threatening to sue his firm for supplies lost when a Baldwin-Lomen ship was sunk by the polar ice pack:

The directors think your friendship
Something fine and great
But God just took the *Silver Wave*
And with it, took your freight.[2]

It was obvious that Baldwin had lost a lot more than had the freight company. The executive decided not to sue.

Arthur Baldwin's strength of character would not let mishaps deter him, which stood him well as 1933 unfurled. Though the year had commenced on an optimistic note, by the end of April, hopes of all concerned had plunged to the opposite end of the scale. Leonard's death was a severe blow to the drive, but the disruption and loss of deer in the storm foretold even greater difficulties. The Lomen company could now expect the expedition to drain their funds of another thirty thousand dollars to keep the drive going for at least another nine months. In addition, the Canadian government suffered from the embarrassment of now having a new reindeer station built with no reindeer in it. This further complicated the original contract signed by the Lapps with the government.

As drawn up by Erling Porsild, this agreement failed to envision that there would be no animals for the immigrant herders to tend after they arrived. Consequently, the part of the agreement that offered the Lapps a bonus of fifty cents a fawn for each fawn born in the spring could not be applied, nor could the offer of reindeer meat and skins sufficient for the Laplanders' own consumption and dress. Another complication as far as the Lapps were concerned was that they had assumed that the drive would be finished before the "expiry" date (June 1, 1933) of the supplementary contract for five hundred dollars that they had signed, whereas it now locked them into staying in the field, with still no end in sight. Thus the Laplanders were concerned about their future, and not in a good frame of mind.

Bahr had no choice but to pasture the reindeer along the Blow River after the storm, as the does were too weak to move anywhere else. They were now in the shadows of the Richardson Mountains, or right in the wolves' front yard. As fawning began, the men got little sleep and were on almost constant patrol. Nerves became frazzled and tempers short. Out on the long, nocturnal watches, a man had plenty of time to brood, and as a result, any imagined slight or indifference while in camp could be nurtured during the protracted lonely periods afield. Real or fancied ills were magnified by the emptiness of the tundra. Bickering between the Lapps and Eskimos ensued. Tornensis, Pulk, and Hatta chose to camp by themselves because of their increasing resentment of Peter and Tommy Wood, whom they contended ran the drive the way they wanted to with little or no consultation from Bahr. The fact that all of the men were existing on meagre rations made the situation even worse. This added to the mental burden of the Lapps, for they were aware that the Wood brothers and other Eskimos from Alaska were making from two to four times more money than were they. Not only were the Lapps irritated over their niggardly wages, but they claimed it stigmatized them as being inferior in the eyes of the Eskimos.[3]

The supply situation was so bad it bordered on the farcical. By May, Bahr was almost desperate:

". . . this country has been very poor, no fox, no caribou, no game, no grub in stores, only a little flour at Aklavik . . . We live monthly on game but you know the game is against the law, too, but have to do something to save life this spring."[4] The fawning season was almost over when Bahr wrote the letter. By then he had moved the herd a little westward from the Blow River to fresher pasture.

Carl Lomen had been informed of the Lapps' general dissatisfaction with field conditions and offered to extend their supplementary pay for another year if they would remain with Bahr. In addition, because a skeleton crew was still needed at the reindeer station, he agreed to pay the wages of the men hired to take the Lapps' place while they were in the field.

Hume transmitted this information to his ranking man in the Mackenzie delta, Dr. Urquhart, and asked him to journey to the reindeer camp to confer with Bahr and find out what exactly the Lapps wanted.

Urquhart travelled by dog team to Shingle Point, and with Bahr as interpreter, went into conference with the Lapps. They told the doctor they were not satisfied with their contract and would not extend it on the same terms when it came up again for renewal on June 1. They wanted supplemental pay for remaining with the herd. Urquhart, in turn, advised them that under the terms of their agreement they were obligated to stay with the deer if so requested. He said their families would be transported to them for the summer, and additional food and supplies would be furnished to them by the government. This appeared to appease the herders. However, Urquhart was not able to get a signed agreement before returning to Aklavik. Even he had reservations about the sincerity of the Laplanders' intentions as to whether they would honour the contract or not. He sent a note to Erling Porsild, and advised him to transport the Lapps' families to the herd come summer, then added laconically: ". . . if their husbands are still working."[5]

Bahr himself had been in the field so long, and separated from his wife, that he was beginning to worry about his financial affairs back home. He was very disturbed over the fact that in three years he had received no notices indicating any money had been deposited into his Seattle bank account. He was worried because payments had to be made on the two apartment houses he owned, and wrote to Ralph Lomen about it:

> If my wife call in to your office, please be kind and explain her. She will write to me. If you haven't paid anything yet, then you have to pay now with six per cent interest compound semi-annually. We are paying six per cent ourselves you know. Hoping this will find you approval.[6]

The adage that when it rains it pours could not be more apropos than as it applied to this reindeer drive. The three Lapps from the Mackenzie ultimately reached the end of their rope and on June 1 quit the drive. They cited poor food and low pay as the reasons. They physically left the camp near Shingle Point and set out on foot across the ice of Mackenzie Bay on a straight line toward the reindeer station. It was an incredible walk. Only a Lapp or an Eskimo ever would have attempted such an extemporaneous hike in that region under such conditions.

Warm, fresh water from the outflow of the Mackenzie River made the bay ice extremely hazardous at that time of the year. Stymied by overflows and open leads in the sea ice, ripped by blizzards, plagued by oscillating temperatures, and constantly aware of the dangers of polar bears,[7] the three Lapps struggled across the wide expanse of ice and treeless islands for twenty-one days before they finally staggered into the reindeer station on the east side of the Mackenzie delta. Once home, and apparently none the worse for wear, they voiced their complaints to Erling Porsild.

Mathis Hatta was the spokesman for the others. He contended that from the time they reached the reindeer camp, they were given poor fare at the dinner table and were on the point of starvation. He said their foot gear and clothing were inadequate, and that Bahr was doing nothing about it. Porsild heard them out and evaluated their grievances.

The ramifications of their departure were not

long in coming as wires began to hum with censure and recrimination. Erling Porsild attempted to explain to the Canadian government what had happened and the reasons for it, based on the Lapps' version of events. Porsild was the man who had hired them and the responsibility for their performance rested on his shoulders. Erling was a hard-working, conscientious young man who believed in doing the best he could for his employer. In fact, he may have been overly zealous in his initial bargaining with the Lapps. The original contract was parsimonious to an extreme and could be attributed to his inexperience, and to basic prejudices. No man is without the latter, though such opinions tend to veer in different directions and interests, and can be both positive and negative in nature. He wrote:

"Lapps have primitive minds, and reasonable latitude must be allowed in dealings with them."[8] Thus, he explained his forbearance concerning the Lapps' abjuration of their contract. Porsild's solution was in keeping with loyalty to his employer. He suggested that the Lomen brothers should reduce the pay of their herders to bring the scale to the level of his Lapps, rather than to increase the Lapps' pay. He neglected to augur the effect of such a proposal on the Lomen employees if the idea was adopted. Plainly, implementation of it would have been disastrous.

Porsild flatly told the Lapps he would fire them for their precipitate action if they did not go back to the drive. Under that threat, the Lapps agreed to go. Erling supplied them with a canoe, and as soon as the ice went out of Mackenzie Bay, he sent the Lapps on their way.

Erling Porsild now thought the situation needed a radical remedy. Despite the apparent earlier vindication of Bahr, he advised Hume he thought the Wood brothers should be fired, and that Bahr be released and a "white man" hired in his place. He was none too complimentary of Bahr:

"Personal contact with Bahr," he wrote, "who in April visited the station one week convinces me he is no longer capable of maintaining discipline or handling the situation. When the drive started, he was too old and since has aged so much he is not even capable of carrying on intelligent conversation."

Hume sent a copy of Porsild's wire to the Lomen brothers with the explanation that as far as the government was concerned, the note was "forwarded without prejudice to existing commitments."[9]

Though Porsild's wire did nothing to improve ethnic harmony, it did achieve concrete results. The Lomens, who had been waffling for three years over hiring someone to oversee Bahr, finally were moved to act. Firstly, Carl Lomen authorized Bahr to dismiss the Wood brothers, though it was more of a request than an order. Ostensibly, Bahr told the two men they were being let go because the drive was nearly over, and their services would therefore not be needed. Also, since the health of the mens' families was not good — Peter had lost his infant daughter, Helen, to pneumonia the previous December, and his wife was not well — Bahr stressed the fact that the Woods' dismissal was more of an accommodation for them than anything else.

However, the real reason the Lomens let them go was to accommodate the Canadians. Since the drive was now close to its destination, it was more important to cater to the customer's wishes than not to do so. The skills of the Woods could be sacrificed to insure harmony among the ultimate permanent herders. Tommy and Peter agreed to leave as soon as a coastwise vessel was available.

Alfred Lomen contacted Dan Crowley, who had done such an excellent job for them in the past, and placed him again in the more active field superintendent's role. Crowley journeyed north from California to Seattle, Vancouver, and Edmonton. Yet even while Dan was in the process of being rehired, the upheaval concerning the reindeer drive continued.

This time the storm swirled around Bob Porsild, who in disgust quit his job at the reindeer station. Bob told Hume that he thought he was slated to be the man in charge of running the reindeer station, not Erling, who had in effect taken over his position. Bob alluded to his brother's poor health as making it impossible for him to handle the heavy physical tasks required to maintain the camp. Besides, he was aware that his brother was angling for a botanist job in Ottawa, and had no intention of remaining at the camp. Bob predicted the reindeer experiment was "foredoomed to failure" for those reasons.

Bob Porsild and his family departed Aklavik up the Mackenzie aboard the riverboat *Distributor* in July. Crowley was told that he had just missed Porsild when he caught the same boat, now headed back downriver, in August.

Crowley's arrival in Aklavik gave another dimension to the reindeer drive. The Lomens now had a permanent appointee on the scene who was a combination of those extra attributes that were sorely needed from the beginning. He was a hardy man, of even disposition, and possessed a natural flair for diplomacy. Crowley displayed these resources immediately on landing at Aklavik, when he met Erling Porsild and his wife on the shore and invited them to lunch aboard the *Distributor*. Their conversation was cordial. Porsild briefed Dan on the status of the drive. He told Crowley the herd had been moved from Shingle Point to Kay Point, where the deer could be watched quite handily along the finite limits of the peninsula which was surrounded on three sides by the Arctic Ocean. The feed there was ample. Porsild informed Crowley that the Lapps' families had joined them. He said he would be going to the drive's location in a month to pick up the wives and children and bring them back for the winter. As far as Porsild knew, everything in the field was running smoothly. Crowley caught a ride on the RCMP boat *St. Roch* when it sailed west for Herschel Island and went ashore at Kay Point to visit the herd. Bahr appeared to be in good spirits. He was happy with the performance of his crew, which now consisted of three Eskimos — Mark Noksana, Terrence Driggs, and the indefatigable Edwin Allen — and the three Canadian Lapps.

Crowley found that Andy Bahr (like Erling Porsild) was overly zealous in protecting his employer's interests:

> He [Bahr] was glad I was going to Herschel and told me to have a talk with the Wood brothers, also to write to you and tell you not to pay Wesley any more money than he had offered him. That he did not hire Wesley until a year ago this spring, and at that time he did not tell him how much wages he was to receive. In settling with him, he paid him at the rate of $25 per month. Although another boy hired about the same time and the same age as Wesley, receives $75 per month. There is no doubt Andrew is working for the best interests of the company, but I am afraid he sometimes drives too sharp a bargain.[10]

Crowley continued on to Herschel Island, where he met the Wood brothers, who were awaiting the arrival of a schooner to take them home. Their version of the relationships in camp was different from that of the Lapps. According to Peter and Tommy, the Canadian Lapps did not have the welfare of the herd at heart. The Wood brothers even went so far as to say they discovered the newcomers had once slaughtered a reindeer and hidden the skin and carcass in the snow prior to carting the meat to camp in their packs and hiding it. They also claimed Hatta, Tornensis, and Pulk concocted some form of "home brew" and would drink it to extreme. They accused Bahr of favouritism towards his countrymen, only one of whom had herded reindeer on a permanent basis in Norway.

Crowley reported that the Woods were completely loyal to Andrew Bahr and had nothing but praise for him as a man doing the very best he could. By way of response to Erling Porsild's charge that the Wood brothers had been running the drive, Crowley observed that if they were, it was in the best interests of the Lomen company. The superintendent assessed the Wood brothers as being "very good reindeer men, honest and willing workers, and had I arrived on the scene ten days earlier, I doubt very much if they would now be going."

The Lomen brothers, on the basis of their own long experience in dealing with herdsmen, sensed a personal antipathy on the part of Erling Porsild towards Andrew Bahr, and decided that Bahr's letters did not appear to reflect any sort of mental or physical collapse as Erling contended. Carl recalled that Porsild had always been against Bahr from the moment he was selected by the Lomens to head the drive. Furthermore, "Porsild has made recommendations to Andrew which, if followed, would have cost us the larger number of the deer now on the drive. The officials at Ottawa are not sold on Porsild, but are in the same position as we are — unable to change their leader at this time."[11]

Only Scandinavians, whose brotherly quarrels among nations are commonly admitted, could comprehend the squabble going on among the various parties involved in the drive. All of the individuals involved fit the "Norsemen" mold in one way or another, including the Wood brothers, who as Inuit, were also intensely proud individuals.

Carl predicted that "Porsild is a stubborn Dane and he will continue to oppose Andrew, lining up his Lapps against our people, and this might cause great losses to the herd and to us."

Lomen did not completely exonerate Bahr, either. He recognized the fact that Bahr may have been delaying the drive to get the extra funds to keep up the payments on his Seattle apartments.

Looking back at the drawn-out row from the present perspective, it is not difficult to discern the overriding cause. It was simply prolonged frustration. The men were losing their "war" with the elements, over which they really had little or no control. After four years of tending the ornery reindeer — already two years more than had been originally estimated, the drive was still susceptible to failure.

Scapegoats are usually sought out when battles are lost. Charges are made and change invoked. A correct formula has to be found to tip the scales in favour of winning through. To do anything to effect a change is better than to do nothing, even if innocent victims get hurt in the process. The Wood brothers were a casualty of this train of thought.

Crowley, as a result of his conversations with Bahr, saw no reason to dismiss him, and retained the trail boss as the titular head of the drive.

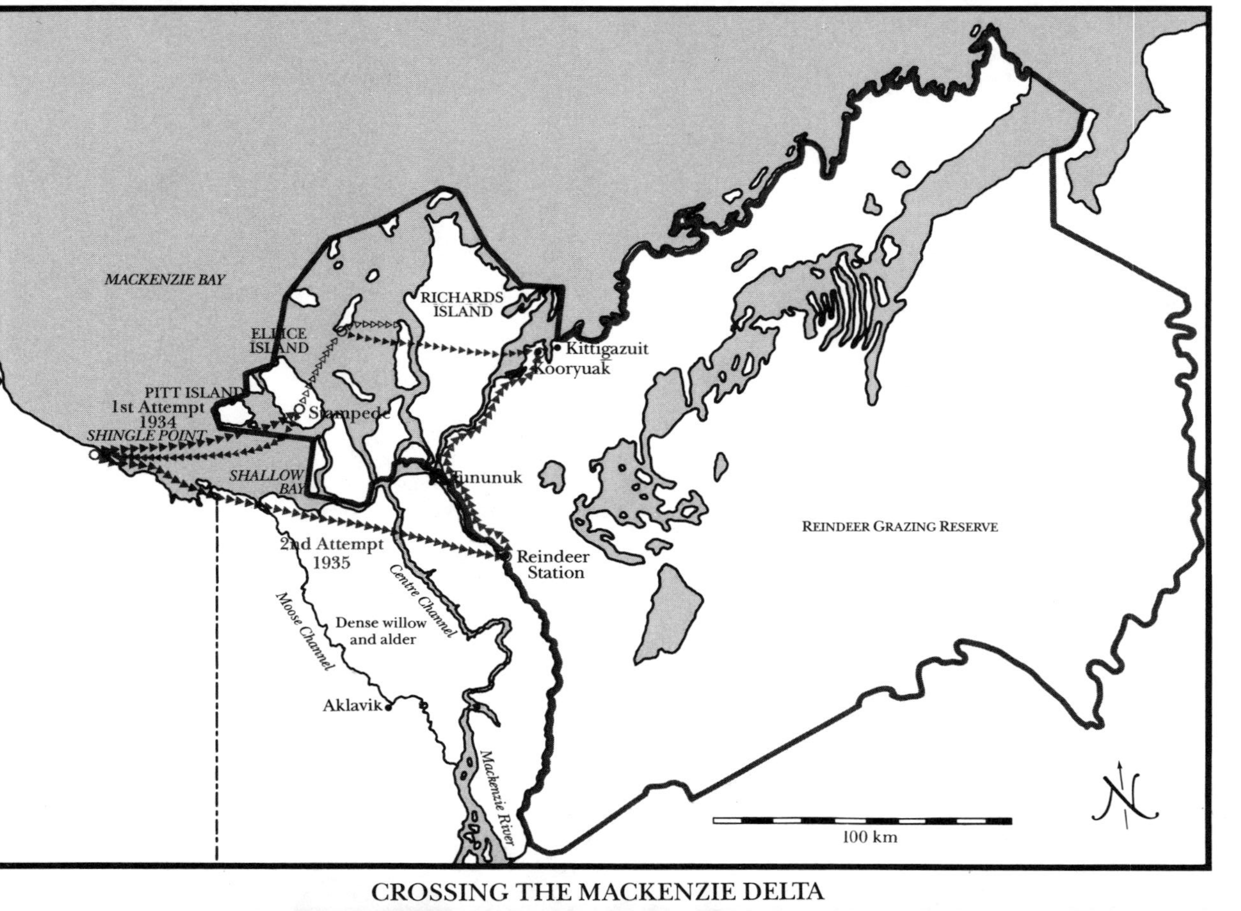

CROSSING THE MACKENZIE DELTA

The Fifth Year

CHAPTER 13

Defeat at Manixa's

Dan Crowley gave an amusing assessment of Bahr's hospitality when he moved in with the old Lapp at Kay Point in August, 1933. He recorded the miserly way in which Bahr parcelled out grub, and in doing so, gave some insight into the reasons the Lapps complained about the food.[1]

The evening Dan arrived, Andrew asked him if he would like a cup of tea. Having travelled all day, Dan agreed it was a good idea. Bahr proceeded to brew some tea and asked Dan if he would like a biscuit.

Crowley nodded.

Bahr said he would get some, and walked out of the tent. In a minute he came back with several.

Crowley looked around for the butter. Noticing this, Bahr asked him if he wanted some. Once more, Crowley nodded.

Bahr got up again, went to the supply tent and brought back a can. He sat down, then looked around the table, and asked Dan if he wanted any milk in his tea, to which his guest replied in the affirmative. Bahr went through the same rigmarole in retrieving the milk. The sugar, perhaps due to "oversight", was already on the table.

Once Crowley settled in with the herders, he was more than satisfied with the work ethic of all of them. He complimented the Eskimos as well as the three Lapps on their industriousness.

Andrew Bahr's summer plan was to graze the herd on the Kay peninsula before pointing it east for the home stretch. Crowley's first day at Kay Point was spent in walking the range and observing the deer. Though widely scattered on the neck of land, the reindeer he did view looked fit.

A few days later, Bahr commenced moving the herd southeast. The deer travelled well, and in a short time the herd had ensconced itself on the upper Kogaruk River. The food was plentiful so Bahr held the herd here through the fall rutting season. Then he would push the animals to Shoalwater Bay east of Shingle Point. The final dash across Mackenzie Bay was to be made from this area.

The Kogaruk was one of their better camps. Situated among some big willows and alders, it was well protected from wind and storms.

The herders grew optimistic as a spell of good weather eased many difficult chores such as the hunt for game, the search for firewood, and keeping watch on the herd. This complacence spilled over into their plans for the future because they had grown so certain they would get through this time. Bahr would return to Seattle, Crowley to California, Mark Noksana and Terrence Driggs to Beechey Point or possibly Aklavik, and Edwin Allen was undecided whether to settle down in Canada or to return to Kobuk village in Alaska. Mathis Hatta, Aslak Tornensis, and Mikkel Pulk were of mixed emotions whether they would stay in Canada or return to Norway. They would make that decision when they renegotiated their contract. Crowley was so sure everything would go all right that he mailed a letter to Ralph Lomen in Seattle asking him to have his suit cleaned and ready for his arrival.

Bahr planned to nudge the herd towards Shingle Point beginning on December 8, but the day before, the weather suddenly turned for the worse. A series of blizzards blew up like a heavy surf to engulf the drainage in a white hell. The blow lasted for eighteen rime-encrusted days, and that is how long it took for the herd to be driven a distance of just twenty miles. During this colossal gale, Crowley saw what to him was one of the most incredible survival episodes he encountered during thirty years in the Arctic. Hatta and Driggs left camp one evening to tend the herd. They did not have dogs with them because they were already engaged in the field. The men by now were camped two miles distant from a tributary up which the herd was pastured. The two men managed to make it to the valley of the creek, then proceeded up stream toward the herd. The peak of the storm struck them half way to their destination, and they became separated. Hatta crawled in among some willows to nestle under his huge parka until the storm blew out. Terrence Driggs, who was wearing a lighter version of outside clothing, decided on another strategy. He was so confident of his sense of smell, he reversed direction on the river trusting that he would be able to pick up the scent of smoke from the camp and find his way to it.

Terrence was drawing on uncounted milleniums of Arctic know-how that had been passed down to him. The Elooktoona (his Eskimo name) family was one of nine in northwest Alaska that were outstanding from the standpoint of wealth and leadership among the Eskimo people. The *oomalik* (leader) came from these families. The *oomaliks* played an important role in inter-village diplomacy, and also in distributing wealth through trading alliances. Terrence's family was one of the first entrusted with a reindeer herd by Sheldon Jackson in keeping with their being the "most articulate and cross-culturally capable among the Eskimo people."[2]

Driggs worked his way slowly downriver. For all intents and purposes, the young Eskimo was rendered blind by the density of the storm. He tested the air like a wolf as he plodded through the vicious, blinding maelstrom. Finally, he detected the odour of smoke, and angled off the river in that direction. Now, however, he was in the utmost danger as compared to when he was on the river where its banks served as a guidon for him. The emission of smoke wavered in its intensity. This forced Driggs to weave his way as he endeavoured to pick up the scent. He proceeded, step by step, until he found Crowley's tent. His sudden appearance rendered Dan speechless with awe. Dan brewed some hot tea for Terrence while the wind roared outside. The velocity of the blow was so devastating that Crowley and Driggs spent the rest of the night holding on to the tent poles in order to keep the canvas from blowing away. Hatta came in the next day, none the worse for his adventure.

The weather cleared up briefly on Christmas Day. That meant the herdsmen were now obliged to bring in the deer that had been scattered by the storm. To do this, they first had to travel on skis over the low hills of that area to lasso sled deer. The task was not an easy one as the temperature had dropped to forty below zero. Preparing the sled deer took an entire day.

The next morning, the sled deer were hitched up and driven out to bring in the rest of the animals. It took another three days to round up the herd before the drive recommenced its relentless walk to the east.

New Year's Eve, the trail drive reached Manixa's. This was no more than a deserted sod house situated on Shoalwater Bay about fifteen miles east of Shingle Point. The shack was broken down with a hole in the roof, a dilapidated door, and walls of logs stacked like a picket fence with much of the chinking blown out.

Manixa[3] was an Eskimo elder who had been recommended to Bahr as a guide for crossing Mackenzie Bay. However, he had abandoned his cabin a year earlier to search out more productive hunting grounds farther east. Bahr, Pulk, and Crowley moved into the cabin and did their best to plug up the gaps in the drafty shelter. This was a futile effort in the depths of night, and their only alternative was to immediately crawl into their sleeping bags to stave off the piercing cold. Even with a fire, they were uncomfortable. Crowley sorely regretted the fact that he had not brought along a toddy to celebrate the arrival of 1934.

Dawn came up the next day like a dying ember at an abandoned campfire. It would be another month before the sun would even reach the earth's rim to cast direct light. In the refracted glow of the invisible orb, the expanse of Mackenzie Bay stretched dimly in the infinite Arctic night. Somehow, the herdsmen would have to push the recalcitrant deer across a twenty-mile stretch of sheer ice to reach the first island. Sixty more miles would then have to be traversed through a labyrinth of isles before they gained the reindeer corrals at Kittigazuit.

A small hitch developed in their plans when Crowley announced that he would not be going across the ice with the herd because he did not possess adequate clothing. Incredible as it may seem, when Crowley had arrived at the camp four months before, he had not bothered to obtain heavy over-garments of fur pants and a heavy parka. Why he neglected to purchase proper gear at one of the trading posts is an enigma. Because of this oversight, Crowley elected to journey directly to the reindeer station, and there await the herd's arrival. He hired a dog team and went to Kittigazuit by way of Aklavik, and to a new, permanent complex built at the tree line sixty miles up the Mackenzie from the original camp. He picked up Erling Porsild at the latter station and the two men proceeded to the old location, where they spent two days repairing and adding panels to the corral. After completing those chores, they holed-up in a cabin, and waited for the arrival of the herd.

Back at Manixa's, Bahr made ready for the dash across the bay. *Manixa's*: a place to inspire the imagination, arising out of the vast untold, unrecorded events of time to capture its tiny space in history, like the O.K. corral, or the Plains of Abraham. Manixa's, the jumping-off point for Bahr's herd, now beginning its fifth year of the most enduring trail drive in the history of North America, and during which the old Lapp had well earned that suitable nickname, "The Arctic Moses". Manixa's, cold and desolate; windswept and lonely; yet prodding the imagination. What ghosts haunted this place? What twist of fate caused men from half way around the world to congregate here while tending two thousand reindeer that had been so long on the trail?

On New Year's day the men hunkered down to rest, and await good weather. Bahr celebrated his fifth New Year's day with the herd. During that time the world had been shaken by financial panic and controversy. May 1931 witnessed the failure of the Austrian Credit-Anstalt which advanced the economic crunch with inevitable bankruptcies that followed. Japan had invaded China's province of Manchuria, in a precursory move of the Pacific war. Hitler was named Chancellor of Germany by Hindenburg in 1933, initiating his rise to power.

North America had seen its share of changes. Mackenzie King was replaced by the Conservative, R. B. Bennett, in 1930 in Canada. Franklin Roosevelt won the presidency for the Democrats in the United States in 1933, and prohibition was repealed in America. Now, at least, Crowley would be able to obtain a legal drink when he returned to Seattle.

January 3, 1934 dawned clear with a three-quarter moon bathing the sunless Arctic sky in its eerie bluish light. Moonbeams played off the snow-covered ice of Mackenzie Bay, providing a surprising radiance to the route the herd was supposed to follow. The mercury read forty below zero. There was no wind to disturb the preternatural silence. At this time of the year, the does were not yet heavy with young, and could be expected to proceed without difficulty.

The sled deer were led out onto the ice and stationed at the head of the herd. Moving to their front were Bahr, and Oliver, an Eskimo elder hired as a guide by Crowley for the push across the bay. Oliver supposedly knew the route that threaded through the islands to the mouth of the Mackenzie River and the destination at Kittigazuit. The regular crew followed, scattered at appropriate intervals: Hatta, Pulk, and Tornensis: the three Eskimos, Driggs, Allen, and Noksana; and an unidentified student from the Shingle Point mission who had been added to help out on the crossing.

Men and dogs were posted at points around the herd that might be vulnerable to a stampede. The men stuffed their pockets with biscuits, dry meat, *muk-tuk*, and any other food that was easily portable, each with his favourite snack. This was it! A tension rippled through the ranks of the herders that was not unlike the strain felt by soldiers going into combat. If the animals faltered on this sortie, it could mean another whole year's delay for the drovers. At worst, the herd might be scattered so far and wide as to be unrecoverable, a complete loss.

Finally, Bahr waved his troops forward, forming a line that stretched for almost a mile. Footing at first was good on the snow-covered ice, and the herd moved easily, without the accordion-like undulations that characterize a herd when part of it bunches up while the other parts stretch out. The warm breath of over two thousand reindeer created a cloud of fog which, under the wan light of the moon, took on its own cerulean glow. The shadowy silhouettes moved like phantoms, now on the ice, and now seemingly suspended above the snowy surface, as if they were no more than a polar mirage that might vanish at the blink of an eye. Adding to the spectral essence of the scene was the winking of the flashlights of the drovers as they signalled messages to each other across the ice. The tiny dots and dashes along the periphery of the herd looked like a bevy of fireflies one sees on a hot summer night in more temperate climates.

Reality was imparted to this polar phantasmagoria by the sudden burst of sounds as the weird parade ventured out onto the frozen bay. Dogs sprang into action, barking; men shouted orders; and the reindeer grunted their protests against the forced march . . . *ogh, ogh, ogh* . . . while the sibilant hiss of expanding and contracting ice under the crunch of thousands of footsteps in the snow reminded one that the spectacle was real.

Progress was satisfactory for the first five hours of the drive, but at that point the deer began to encounter patches of ice swept bare and polished to a glaze by the storm winds of the preceding weeks. A reindeer's hooves, though proportionately large and specialized for navigating swamps in the summer and snow in winter, are not suited for crossing glare ice because they contract, giving them no traction. Realizing the animals would not venture onto these patches of ice, Bahr instructed Oliver to plan detours around them. In fulfilling this need, a crazy zig-zag path had to be followed from one patch of snow to the next, which doubled the distance the herd was forced to travel. The animals were overly tired by the time they reached a small island, the first isle some fifteen hours into the drive. The forage was poor, but there was enough food to keep the deer manageable.

Bahr let the herders and the animals rest for two hours before giving the order to move on. At the same time, he instructed Oliver to avoid willow clumps in which the deer might become entangled and unruly. Thirty hours into the journey, the tired herd struggled onto yet another island. Bahr hoped this outcrop would carry enough food to sustain the herd. There was plenty of grass, but it was dried out and virtually of no nutritional value. The deer roamed about, seemingly satisfied with what there was and commenced to graze.

The men were tuckered out after having plodded through the raw, bone-chilling cold while the planet whirled one complete turn on its axis. Their clothes were soaked with sweat, and stuck clam-like to their skin from the tremendous physical effort. The wet clothes fostered a chilling effect on the men, and when the temperature dropped another ten degrees to fifty below zero, their condition assumed critical proportions. One of the Lapps who was wearing unsuitable mittens froze his hands. As a result, he could not feed himself or even hold a cup of tea without help. Another Lapp suffered a badly sprained back when a sled deer lurched, knocking him over.

The accidents and the run-down condition of the herders forced Bahr to call a halt. He chanced putting up a tent because he had no choice if the men were to get warmed up: half a hundred degrees below zero was nothing to fool with. If they did not dry out their clothes and take on food and liquid, their metabolic reservoir would be drained dry and they would begin to freeze. They built a fire in their small rectangular stove, and crammed it full of willow sticks. That was enough to warm them up. They drank hot tea, and brewed chunks of stew that had been frozen before they started.

Bahr wanted someone to watch the herd, but the men, including Bahr himself, were so thoroughly exhausted, he entrusted the fate of the herd to luck. Indeed, the deer seemed to be contented, browsing quietly.

It was then that the mischievous boreal gods played their trump card. A southwest wind sprang up. It was not intense initially, but the scent of their own passage and the lure of feed on the distant mainland that lay behind them caused the panic-prone deer to turn and head en masse into the wind and back the way they had come.

Bahr and his men had been resting for two hours when one man went out to check the herd to see what sort of condition it was in. He arrived in time to see the last few rumps disappear into the rising storm. The nightmare of drovers from time immemorial had come to pass: two thousand deer and more, fractious from the long drive and too little food, had bolted for the mainland. Bahr sent the four Eskimos racing after the irrational creatures to turn them around while the Lapps remained, holding one hundred of the herd that had not bolted, as well as thirteen sled deer.

The Inuit herders did their best to catch up, but patches of glare ice that diverted the animals on the way across served the same purpose on the way back. Without the constraining herders, the deer scattered in all directions. The storm kept building in intensity until it became what the natives called an *agnik*: a full-fledged blizzard. Noksana, Driggs, and Allen now had to worry more about saving themselves than the deer. If they became disoriented on the ice and missed the island, they could easily freeze to death. Helped by the dependable noses of their dogs, one by one the four men eventually drifted into Bahr's camp up to four hours later.

In the meantime, Bahr had consigned to the Lapps the task of driving the 100 reindeer that had not run off twenty miles to Richards Island. He figured if he could get the animals to that island, which had plenty of desirable forage, they would stay there. The storm, by now, had evolved into an Arctic hurricane. The Lapps, handicapped by their injuries, lost track of the small herd in the maelstrom, but kept going toward Richards Island, which they reached safely with the thirteen sled deer.

After the Eskimos had rested, they decided, the next morning, to head for Shingle Point, looking for deer as they proceeded across the ice. Their hike proved to be yet another severe test of endurance because they had to walk into the teeth of the continuing gale, which took its toll. Terrence Driggs froze toes on both feet, and all of the men suffered frostbitten cheeks. They reached Shingle Point safely, but Bahr and Oliver, who were expected to follow them, did not arrive. A day passed, and another, and then three. The people of Shingle Point began to worry about the fate of the two men. To be footloose that long on the Arctic Ocean in a howling blizzard was to defy fate.

Back at the original camp, Oliver had told Bahr there were people living on Kendall Island, from whom they could get supplies. Bahr suggested Oliver take the dog team and go there, but the elderly man did not want to travel alone. The trail boss agreed to go with him and they set out in the storm. The team moved slowly as the dogs were already tired from continuous travel with little rest. Oliver estimated they would reach the island in four hours.

Bahr and Oliver almost expired from the combination of cold and wind as they made their way toward the sanctuary which was situated on the far northern fringe of the Mackenzie delta. Bahr parodied his own intense discomfort in a letter: "I shiver, one could hear my teeth one hundred feet from me."[4]

After travelling for twenty-four hours, they came upon a substantial-looking shelter, virtually a house rather than a cabin. The two men staggered into the refuge, more dead than alive. There was no one around, but plenty of wood was available. They built a fire in the stove and in a short time were comfortably warm. Bahr commented: "Strip off our ice and wet clothes and turn all our dogs loose. Fed them good on fish and hung up all our clothes to dry and afterward got to bed."

They remained in the house four days while they waited for the storm to abate. During this time the residents, Denis Araktok and Joe Illisiak, returned. Since the welcome mat was always out among Inuit, the owners were hospitable to the visitors and sold Bahr whatever supplies they could spare. In addition, one of their dog teams was hired by Bahr to help haul supplies to their island camp site. From there, it took two night camps before Bahr and Oliver made it back to Shingle Point and their mates. The people of the mission were much relieved to see them.

In the next few days, as the men recovered from the ordeal of the crossing, the harsh realization began to sink in, that the Arctic winds seemed to have snatched victory from them while they were almost in sight of their destination. From force of habit they began to prepare to go again in search of the deer, hardly taking time to ask whether or not there were any left to bring in. Several small bands that had been seen, disoriented and heading out to sea, were later unaccounted for, and presumed to have been lost. Others were met by wolves as they came off the ice, and, if not killed on the spot, were chased into the Richardson Mountains where they disappeared.

Luckily, most of the herd was found intact along the banks of the Blow River only a few miles east from where the last stage of the drive had begun.

The drovers found good feed for the deer farther east along Moose Channel of the Mackenzie and pastured them there. Then, during the next few weeks the herders travelled far and wide, bringing in strays. By the time they were satisfied they had collected all the deer within a reasonable distance, the animals were too run-down to attempt the crossing again before the spring thaw. And then it would be too late until summer and fall had passed and winter had returned again. Several days of an evil wind had just added another year to the drive. To a man, the drovers cursed the Arctic, blasphemed the winds, and rued the day they had ever set out on such an expedition.

Dan Crowley, in a letter to Ralph Lomen explaining the setback, blamed Bahr's lack of organizational ability as the principal cause for the disaster. He vowed it would not happen again. Dan swore that the next time the route would be carefully mapped and staked out in advance, with food caches placed at strategic locations along the way, and lichen picked, bagged, and towed on sleds to make sure the deer had enough food.

Crowley conceded that the drive would have to be deferred to next winter, and since the herd was down to around fourteen hundred deer, all they could hope for was a good fawn crop in April and May of this year, 1934, to bring the numbers back to where they had been before the stampede.

Andrew Bahr suspected he was being made the scapegoat of the disaster by Crowley, and did his best to present his own side of the story to the Lomens in a letter dispatched on March 18, 1934. He had warned Crowley in a not unfriendly debate that the drive across Mackenzie Bay should not have been attempted before February or March because of the short days and the likelihood that the ice would have been swept clear of snow. No one had supported him in this except the Lapp, Aslak Tornensis. Bahr wrote: "I was alone, such fool." The trail boss had, in fact, added an ominous note in his argument against crossing the ice in the cold months of December and January, when he said: "I told Mr. Crowley we are liable to lost whole drive and freeze ourselves dead too."[5]

The Lomen brothers received the discouraging news of the stampede with creditable forbearance. They were generally tolerant of the many diverse opinions that came to their eyes and ears, and were seldom critical of Bahr, Crowley, the Porsild brothers, or other men in the field. When they wanted something done, they usually expressed their wishes in the form of a suggestion, not a dictate. Their own years in the field furnished them with a knowledgeable empathy for the herders and their difficulties. However, the Lomens were having their own share of troubles which seemed to multiply in the face of the misfortunes of the drive.

The adage that adversity breeds adversity as success does success, though of questionable logic, surely held true for the Lomens in the aftermath of the defeat at Mackenzie Bay.

The retreat in disarray to the mainland served to focus worrisome eyes on the drive. The Canadian government decided it would be in its own best interest to review its contract with the Lomen corporation and postulate on its terms, if by chance the venture failed and the Lomens defaulted. Government attorneys were called in to prepare a legal brief that would cover all eventualities as well as answer several specific questions about the drive, one being the consequences if the Lomen company simply abandoned the herd. Hume wondered whether the government should assume proportional responsibility, since it had already advanced payment to the Lomen company.

Attorneys, after carefully examining the uncomplicated document, advised Hume that they should, and gave an example. If the government did have to take over the herd, and the Lomens were due any funds after the remaining deer were rounded up and counted, they would be entitled to the balance, less expenses incurred. The reverse would hold true if the reindeer count was under the equivalent sum already advanced to the Lomen corporation.

It was obvious that the Lomens had taken a tremendous loss as the result of the failure at Mackenzie Bay. The dollar value of the six hundred lost deer amounted to thirty-nine thousand dollars. In view of this, and based on a plan advanced by Crowley, the Lomens asked the Canadian government if they could fill out the depleted herd with deer purchased from Inuit along the coast.

This request was forwarded to Erling Porsild, who had travelled to Ottawa to confer with Hume about the ill fortune of the reindeer drive. Erling's previous trip along the coast now served him well because he had taken measurements of the deer and found them to be considerably undersized as compared to the Tunguse strain making up the reindeer of the drive. He advised the government to turn down the Lomen request. They accepted the refusal without argument. They could do nothing about it anyway, and there were still suspicions among the coastal Inuit (sometimes fomented pharisaically by the mission teachers) that the Lomens would cheat native herders if given the chance. Other Eskimo ranchers worried that if the Lomen herders tried to round up strays, they would, wittingly or not, sweep up many non-Lomen deer in the process. As it turned out, only thirteen deer eventually delivered at the Mackenzie displayed another owner's ear marks, a remarkably low level of "contamination" after a five-year trail drive.

Other problems beset the Lomens as 1934 progressed, including a fire which destroyed a couple of city blocks in downtown Nome. Almost everything the Lomens owned went up in the conflagration, including their stores, offices, and the home of one of the brothers. As a consequence, they were slow in paying some of the vouchers that had accrued with Hudson's Bay and other companies along the coast. This served to add to the growing concern over whether the company would hold together long enough to complete the drive and pay the outstanding bills.

The fact that hearings on the industry were being held in Washington, D. C., where Carl Lomen was spending more and more time, was another needle in the side of the operation. This, too, worried the Canadian government which requested its embassy in Washington to ascertain the status of the reindeer industry in Alaska. Lyman S. Brewster, overseer of the industry for the United States government in the Alaska territory, was pessimistic about the future. The industry was in a state of decline, with meat costing now six cents a pound to produce, and only four cents a pound being paid on the dock in Seattle. He said the Depression had taken the floor out of the market, and with beef selling at rock bottom prices, cattlemen were in no mood to be receptive to a competitor. He surmised that the ultimate result would be a buy-out of all private holdings of deer by the United States government with the idea of preserving "the industry solely as a source of supply of food and clothing for the exclusive use of the Eskimos and natives of Alaska."[6] Or, as the Canadian report summed it up, the reindeer meat operations in Alaska for purposes of export looked to be on the verge of collapse.

This report could not have done anything but make Canada's Interior Department wonder if they had purchased a huge "pig in a poke". The original basis for Canadian optimism had been the two decades of success of the reindeer industry in Alaska. If there was no market in which to sell the animal products, the purpose for which the industry was being built, that of earning income for the Eskimos, would be destroyed. The Canadians faced the burden of endless subsidies that would be needed to maintain the herd they had purchased, once it was delivered. The reindeer would, of course, provide a steady source of food for the native people, and prevent the endemic bouts of starvation, which was also part of the original intent, but the project was starting to look like a boondoggle. Nonetheless, whether a "pig in a poke" or not, the Canadian government was committed to receiving the deer.

CHAPTER 14

The Final Crossing

Andrew Bahr let the animals gain strength on the Moose Channel pasturage east of the Blow River through the spring of 1934. Moderate weather prevailed when the fawn crop came in. With almost all of the does delivering a fawn, and most of them surviving because of the good weather, one thousand deer were added to the herd.

Bahr then shifted the reindeer to Kay Point as he had done the year before. He found the feed to be bountiful there, and the snow soft. Contrary to more harsh years, it was easy for the deer to dig down to get forage.

The animals thrived, and in a rough count, numbered about twenty-four hundred head. This placed the Lomens into a cash receiving position (relative to the partial payments made so far) rather than a reimbursement situation, when and if the reindeer were successfully delivered.

Crowley, who had rejoined the herd after the debacle of the crossing, though appreciative of the fine crop of fawns, was plainly disturbed by one detrimental aspect of the good weather that summer, this being the fog that swept in from the Arctic Ocean. Warmth translated into fog when the rays of the summer sun warmed up the cold water of the polar sea. The mist swirled in over the coastline to envelop the land in its gray shroud, rendering the drovers blind to the stealthy approaches of the ever-persistent wolves.

Constant watch and continual alertness managed to keep losses from wolves relatively light but the nuisance of their raids proved tiring to the drovers who had to plod over the soggy muskeg to round up the herd after each sortie. Their energy was sapped and their alertness less keen. In one instance, Aslak Tornensis thought he saw a wolf among the herd and snapped off a shot in the misty light, killing the animal. When he walked up to examine the dead predator it turned out to be Red, one of the herd dogs.

Dan Crowley put in part of the summer at Herschel Island, waiting on the arrival of Captain Pedersen and his schooner, the *Patterson*. Planning the logistics for next winter's crossing, he purchased seven months of supplies which he calculated would last the herders through March 1935. (Captain Pedersen's opinion was that a crossing should not be attempted before February, thus supporting Bahr's earlier arguments.) Beyond that date Dan made no plans, because to him such an eventuality was too untenable to face. If they failed to reach the corrals through that springtime "window", it was highly doubtful that the drive would continue. The Lomens themselves had mentioned this possibility to their backer, Arthur Baldwin. Even now, serious consideration was being given to some sort of cash settlement with the Canadian government, whereby the reindeer would be turned over to the Canadians on the west side of the Mackenzie delta.

The Canadian government worried about this eventuality also, and authorized Erling Porsild to investigate various ways of moving the deer to Kittigazuit. One option was to herd the animals onto a barge and float them in several relays across the bay. Porsild estimated that as many as one thousand deer could be moved at one time by barge. This idea, however, was never extensively pursued because of the logistical problems involved. Barges were in demand for other activities, and even if one was obtained, there was always the chance ice floes could prevent its use, or capsize it.

Erling also, of course, re-evaluated the possibility of driving the herd across the bay as Bahr had attempted. He deemed it practical if enough help could be mustered to control the reindeer during the crossing.

The Lapps' contract expired on July 19, while

they were in the field with the herd at Kay Point. Tornensis, Pulk, and Hatta opted to leave Bahr's camp — albeit this time with due notice — and return to Kittigazuit, their purpose being to amend the provisions of the contract that did not apply because they were not at the reindeer station, and then return.

Crowley exhibited some concern when the Lapps had not returned after a month's absence: "I do not see how the Canadian government can afford to leave them go at this time. It would be quite a blow to us if they do not return, as they are good reindeer men and can not be replaced. However, if we have to we can get along without them."[1]

Kay Point was a good spot. The breezes from the Arctic Ocean furnished welcome relief from mosquitoes throughout the summer. Alternatives to the menu of the herders were provided by a large population of wild fowl that nested in the vicinity. Occasionally they would obtain bigger game. Edwin Allen and Mark Noksana, while returning from King Point with a boat for transferring supplies and gear, shot two caribou, which were a welcome change to canned products.

The first snows fell in mid-August, and in sufficient depth to stick on the distant foothills. A warm spell melted off most of the white mantle along the shore line, but this thaw abruptly came to an end on September 16, when the polar ice pack moved in overnight to cover the sea from horizon to horizon. Two days later the small bay on which the drovers were camped froze thick enough for them to load up their sleds and shift the camp across its one-mile expanse to set up operations on the far shore. Snow blew in, covered the ground, and stuck! It looked like winter had descended on the herd once more.

The fickle Arctic had yet another trick to play — but this one was in the drive's favour. A few days after the second freeze up, a chinook engulfed the bay and the camp, thawing the snow and blowing the floe ice out to sea. The mild weather held, and as a result, provided ideal conditions for the fall rut which extended from late August to October. With the herd docile and well fed, it insured an excellent fawn crop the following spring.

Bahr, Crowley, and the others were still anxiously awaiting the Lapps' return. Meanwhile, at the reindeer station, Erling Porsild was driving a hard bargain in negotiating the new contract desired by the Lapps. He admitted their demands were not unreasonable in view of the conditions under which they had lived over the preceding years, but refused to put their pay on a par with the one-hundred-dollar-a-month salary of the Alaskan Eskimos.

Though satisfied with the work of Mikkel Pulk and Aslak Tornensis, Porsild was not fully satisfied with Mathis Hatta, blaming him for much of the trouble and dissatisfaction among his co-workers, and hinted that he should resign. Porsild's observation indirectly supported the Wood brothers' complaints earlier about their relations with the Lapp contingent from Canada; Hatta may have been the culprit about whom they were griping. Hatta's influence, no matter what his faults, resulted in Porsild's grudging acquiescence to a raise in the Lapps' base pay from forty to sixty dollars a month, plus free schooling for their children in Aklavik, and the Lapps rejoined the reindeer drive in December 1934.

The dialogue continued between Crowley and Bahr with respect to the strategy they would employ to cross Mackenzie Bay. Crowley wanted to place two relief camps along the route. Fresh herders would await the drive at each camp and replace drovers from the preceding phase. Dan also insisted that deer moss collected on the mainland be stored at each camp and fed to the deer in the course of the drive. In addition, Dan wanted to gamble on taking a route closer inshore rather than to point the herd far out onto the open ice of Mackenzie Bay.

Bahr, on the other hand, saw such precautions as a waste of time and money. Said Bahr: "I tell him that is all unnecessary and waste expense. We don't need no stake trails and no stations but we need proper season for crossing. That's all we need and we should not bother the herd . . . but hold the herd in the best feeding grounds until February and then go across without any fuss in safety."[2]

Dan Crowley was amazed that Bahr could be so phlegmatic about the crossing, especially after having already failed twice in striving to achieve it. In

Dan's opinion, the previous failures were due to one fact only: poor organization, particularly with reference to the failed attempt of the year before. The drive was lost when the men took a break and left the herd — it was as simple as that.

Bahr, at first, was adamantly against their trying to cross Mackenzie Bay in November or December, though he slowly acceded to Crowley's wishes as his superior. But Crowley, too, would have lessons to learn about the vagaries of the Arctic weather.

Late in November the drive moved eastward again toward Manixa's in anticipation of the dash across the bay to the east side of the delta. Initially, climatic conditions were perfect: the bay froze over, and simultaneously snow came down to deposit the necessary footing for the deer. Then the weather turned clear; the moon was due full at the proper time, and with the clear sky would provide maximum light. In the three years Bahr and his men had been trying to move the deer across the bay, the elements had never been so generous. If there was ever a time to go, this was it.

Ironically, Crowley and Bahr found themselves again at Manixa's on New Year's Eve. Once more they were bivouacked in the broken-down dwelling with the hole in the roof and the driftwood walls. Now, instead of three men being crammed into the cabin at the break of the new year, there were four, in addition to six dogs! Shepherd dogs, the prima donnas of the drive, rated quarters right along with their masters, while the Inuit members of the crew took bunks with relatives at Shingle Point.

Crowley's memory did not have to be acute to recall the previous New Year at Manixa's when the mercury fell so low it bottomed out and was indistinguishable on the thermometer. Now they were more comfortable, and this time Dan had taken the precaution to have liquor in his possession. The birth of 1935 would be celebrated in style.

"I'll never forget last year," Crowley wrote, "as the wind came through the chinks in the logs . . . three of us so sick with cold we should have been in bed, and not a drop of *medicine* in camp."[3]

If anyone had forgotten the shack after the first New Year's spent there, he certainly would not forget the second. Though more comfortable this year from a physical standpoint, the herders were far from being at ease. The tedium of the drive was getting to them. Probably the worst part about their situation was they were so near to their destination in distance, but still so far in terms of the major, critical task still to be done.

Mother nature became fickle: an eight-day thaw set in, melting all of the snow with the exception of deep drifts, and leaving the ice of the bay barren. The weather held clear with little or no wind. These were excellent conditions, but not for their task. Without snow to give traction, the reindeer could not be budged from the shore.

How many reindeer drives had ever arrived at the

Mackenzie delta in December hoping for snow as footing to cross the bay; and how often had there ever been a thaw at that time of year to take it away?

Each morning Crowley stood looking dumbly at the glare ice of the bay, irked by the fact that he could do nothing about it. In frustration, he wrote: "It would be just my luck to run into such a d — — winter as this. In memory of the oldest inhabitant, they have never had anything like it before."

Mikkel Pulk voiced the frustrations of all of them when he wrote: "We cannot help getting tired waiting for the reindeer to get across the river. The time seems to drag terribly, and it does not look like we will get across this year either."[4]

Crowley, thoroughly depressed by the unfathomable thaw and contrary elements at that time, was a master of understatement in his diary. "I will have to admit that this country, and the conditions under which I have been living, are beginning to get my goat."[5]

The Lapps were anxious to get home and the Eskimos, too, had had enough. Grippe almost incapacitated Bahr, as he suffered from excruciating headaches and a cough. Even Erling Porsild complained back at the reindeer station: "I have suffered more this winter from rheumatism or lumbago than in any previous winter."

There seemed to be an unspoken agreement among all of Lomen's crew that if the crossing was not successful this time around, the drive would end at Manixa's as far as they were concerned.

Possibly the Lomens would hire another crew, but their financial prospects were as gloomy as the mood of the men on the drive. As a fall-back position, the company was soliciting producers of dog food to see if they would purchase thousands of pounds of first-class reindeer meat they could not sell. In a letter to Dan, Ralph reported that four of the leading dog food brands in the United States did an aggregate business of forty million dollars in 1933. "All we want is a million from each of them and we will be happy."[6]

The date of the January full moon passed, and still no snow had fallen to cover the ice. The next full moon would not be until mid-February. The men waited. Tension continued to build and the frustrations deepened as the snowless skies persisted. Drought-ridden farmers praying for rain could not have been any more intent than the drovers wishing for snow.

Erling Porsild's anxiety continued to build at the reindeer station. He was apprehensive because he had received several offers of jobs as a botanist, and if he did not get back to Ottawa for the interviews, he might not be hired at all.

Crowley was equally impatient. He prowled the proposed route distributing sacks of lichen for the deer, and canned food for the men at selected locations along the way. He had also implanted sticks marking the route across the ice. Dan was taking no chances. If anyone among the drovers wanted to complete the drive, he did. He was over fifty, and had been in the field for eighteen months. Plainly, it was now or never.

Finally, the break came. A foot of the white crystals fell in the last week of January. Subsequent squalls in the next several weeks added to the layer of snow that covered the ice of the bay making the depth suitable for the attempt.

On February 18, the exodus set out again from Manixa's. The line of deer filed out onto the ice gingerly, testing the footing as they plodded toward the obscure horizon. Imperceptibly, almost at the minute the deer's hooves touched the ice, a breeze sprang up. Were the trickster gods preparing yet another gigantic joke to play on the drovers? Ignoring the stiffening breeze, Bahr, Crowley, and the herdsmen refused to be intimidated and pressed the deer forward.

This time they followed the edge of the delta more closely as the drive lurched into the history books. Now resting, now feeding, and then parading forward, twenty-four hundred reindeer picked their way across the ice of the bay under the gaudy lights of the aurora borealis and the illumination of a "reindeer moon". The herd successfully traversed the unsheltered stretch of Mackenzie Bay and reached Ellice Island in good condition. That night, under rotating watches of the herders, the deer were contained in a refuge provided by the steep banks of the narrow Tikdalik River. The next morning the drive commenced again, weaving among the islands of the delta. Another night was spent on the trail, pushing the animals to the limit of their endurance. Frequent stops were made during which reindeer moss was unloaded from sleds and fed to the animals, restoring their strength.

Late on the third day Bahr called for a rest. The herd was on the ice, and in sight of Richards Island, but the trail boss realized they were just too tired to go on. In fact, they were so played out, the entire lot of them lay down on the ice. This was a phenomenon seldom witnessed by the herders.

After several hours, Bahr moved them forward again, the drovers and dogs allowing for no digressions on the part of the deer. Soon the splay-hoofed creatures sniffed the odour of lichen that grew in profusion on Richards Island, and their gait speeded up. They climbed the steep banks of the isle and began to graze contentedly as there was plenty of edible forage. They were now only thirty miles from the corrals at Kittigazuit. It was February 21, 1935. The men had lost only two deer during the crossing, making it a truly remarkable achievement by any measure.

Crowley and Bahr decided to hold the herd near the tiny settlement at Tununuk on the East Channel of the Mackenzie until the deer had gained strength and were ready to proceed on the last leg of the journey.

A week went by. The men then headed the deer to the reindeer station where they were run through the chutes on March 6, 1935. A total of 2,370 deer were counted, with 1,498 of them being females. This figure, at sixty per cent, was a higher and more satisfactory ratio than had been expected.[7] Andrew Bahr and his men had won.

The drive was over, but the haggling was not. Both Porsild and Crowley were cranky after the wind-up of the trail drive. Each was loyal to his employer and did his best to represent those interests in a favourable way. Crowley wanted one hundred dollars for each of the six reindeer dogs. Porsild contended they were too old to be worth that much and offered fifty dollars.

A lone female caribou that had been with the drive for a considerable amount of time was not counted by Porsild. Crowley felt that she should have been.

Another dispute arose over the sled deer that had been turned loose on Richards Island by the Lapps during the storm of the previous year, and later caught and taken to the station. Crowley figured they were as much a part of the herd as those already passed through the chutes, and should be counted. Erling Porsild, though acknowledging the reasonableness of that request, foresaw problems if he was expected to pay for every straggler that popped up over the coming months, and turned Crowley down.

They disputed the price to be paid for the

reindeer sleds, which had been made in Seattle and were much too heavy for regular use. The bulky sleds had been a continuing source of complaints from members of the drive since the day it started. Crowley asked twenty-five dollars for each sled. Porsild countered that he could build them himself for ten dollars less.

The fears of missionaries that the Lomen herd would seriously deplete the stocks of the native reindeer ranchers along the coast of the Arctic Ocean proved to be ungrounded. The thirteen non-Lomen strays that were counted in the final tally were accepted by Porsild. Since it was adjudged that some of the uncaptured Lomen strays joined various herds that were grazed along the coast of the Arctic Ocean over the course of the drive, it probably more than balanced the difference.

Because a fawn crop of 811 was born shortly after the arrival of the herd at the reindeer corrals (for which Canada did not have to pay), the Canadian government generously readjusted Porsild's estimates and credited the Lomens with the prices Crowley had sought for the dogs and sleds, and also credited them with the sled deer strays.

Including the initial and interim payments, and the final pay-out of $33,900, the government of Canada paid a total of $146,400 to the Lomen company for bringing in the 2,300 deer.

Thus ended the longest-lasting trail drive in the history of North America, and, undoubtedly, the most remarkable. It had featured semi-wild animals that most North Americans had never seen, and whose meat they had never tasted. It had taken whites and natives of four countries — Canada, the United States, Norway, and Denmark — to succeed, and had involved governments at federal, state, and territorial levels. Now the future of the northern aboriginal peoples in the delta area would be more secure.

EPILOGUE

Shortly after the delivery of the herd and final settlement of all costs, Erling Porsild took a job with the National Museum of Canada as a specialist in his field of botany, where he spent the rest of his life. He wrote one of the definitive books on Arctic plant life, and won many awards for his work.

Andrew Bahr returned to his home in Seattle where festivities held for him by the city included an "Andy Bahr Day". However, all of the news was not good. He lost his two apartment houses for non-payment on his loans, but salvaged enough to live in comfort until his death ten years later. When asked how he felt about the loss of his investments, Bahr shrugged and explained that it mattered little as compared to the fact that he had obtained papers and was a United States citizen. For Andrew Bahr, that counted more than anything.

The Lomen brothers' great dream was shattered in 1937 when the United States government took over the reindeer industry in Alaska. From that time on, no white man, not even Lapps, could own a female reindeer. The Lomens' contention that private enterprise was crucial to the industry for establishing markets proved at least partially correct as the entire industry collapsed shortly after they were forced out of it. Twenty years later, the number of deer had dwindled from three-quarters of a million head to several thousand. The reindeer industry did not win its way back to prominence in Alaska until the 1980s, when it regained lost importance and now, with over fifty thousand animals, supplies the needs of that area's expanded population.

In Canada, after a slow start, general indifference on the part of government and disinterest by natives, the herd was turned over to private enterprise where it has thrived and grown into a million-dollar industry under the management of a native Eskimo, William Nasogaluak. His own private herd numbered approximately eight thousand deer in 1987.[1]

Thus, the vision of the pioneers of the region has been partially fulfilled. The work of the men who persevered for over five years on the trail was not in vain.

ENDNOTES

CHAPTER 1 (p.1)

1. See *Overland to Starvation Cove* by Heinrich Klutschak, trans. and edited by William Barr (Toronto: University of Toronto Press, 1987).
2. The Commission members included chairman John Gunion Rutherford of the Canadian Board of Railway Commissioners; James Stanley McLean, Harris Abattoir Company (later Canada Packers); James B. Harkin, Commissioner of Dominion Parks, and Vilhjalmur Stefansson, Explorer.
3. *Book of the Eskimos*, Peter Freuchen (Cleveland: World Publishing Company, 1961).
4. Nuligak, an Eskimo who published his autobiography, *I, Nuligak* in 1966, described one of these hunts in which they used kayaks almost the way a cowboy used horses, to drive belugas up onto sandbars. Once the whales had beached themselves in the shallow water, they were harpooned. Nuligak recalls that on one hunt, three hundred and fifty whales were taken.
5. Testimony, April 29, 1925.

CHAPTER 2 (p.18)

1. Brooklyn *Daily Times*, March 20, 1926.
2. Letter, Finnie to Leonard Baldwin, Aug. 22, 1925.
3. Letter, Erling Porsild to O. S. Finnie, Dec. 12, 1926.
4. Porsild to Finnie, July 13, 1927.

5. An example is mentioned by Nuligak in his previously mentioned autobiography. In July 1929, he sold his winter fur catch for $2,799. Calculated on a monthly basis, this was twice the salary of an Alaskan reindeer herder, and more than either of the Porsild brothers' base pay. Nuligak met Finnie at that time because the director had come down river to offer five dollars to each Eskimo as "treaty money". Nuligak spurned the offer as did most of the Inuit. He suggested instead that the "white chief" establish an overall fund to help the needy. In a sense, the reindeer program's purpose was to do just what Nuligak asked.
6. Porsild to Finnie, April 18, 1927.

CHAPTER 3 (p.41)

1. Memo, Erling Porsild to W. W. Cory, Oct. 31, 1928.
2. *Fifty Years in Alaska*, Carl Lomen (David McKay, 1954) p. 250–51.
3. Eielson, with Sir Hubert Wilkens, was the first pilot to fly the Arctic Circle route from Alaska to Europe. The wreck was not discovered until late January. Both Eielson and Borland were dead.

CHAPTER 4 (p.65)

1. Report, W. B. Miller to L. J. Palmer, Feb. 26, 1930. The following two excerpts are also from this report.
2. This plan, at best, was a vague one. If the herd had left in mid-October as first planned, they would have reached the Kobuk by year's end, and have been far beyond the Kobuk by fawning time. But judging by Bahr's preoccupation with the Kobuk cache before the drive even started, it is doubtful that he ever considered going farther than that by fawning time in April and May, 1930.

CHAPTER 5 (p.87)

1. Letter, Bob Porsild to O. S. Finnie, June 3, 1930.
2. Letter, Bob Porsild to O. S. Finnie, Aug. 26, 1930.
3. Letter, Bob Porsild to O. S. Finnie, Nov. 10, 1930.
4. Whitehorse *Star*, no date.
5. Whitehorse *Star*, no date.

CHAPTER 6 (p.102)

1. Letter, Andrew Bahr to Alfred Lomen, March 22, 1930.
2. Letter, Carl Lomen to Mike Nilluka, Sept. 20, 1930.
3. Letter, Mike Nilluka to Carl Lomen, Sept. 29, 1930.
4. Letter, Dan Crowley to G. J. Lomen, Sept. 21, 1930.

CHAPTER 7 (p.117)

1. Letter, Andrew Bahr to Alfred Lomen, Jan. 3, 1931 (and subsequent 2 quotes).
2. Letter, Andrew Bahr to Alfred Lomen, March 9, 1931.
3. Letter, Dan Crowley to Alfred Lomen, April 9, 1931. Snow takes on a blue tint when seen from the air. Any break in the snow, such as animal tracks, appear white.
   The next two quotations are from this same report.

CHAPTER 8 (p.140)

1. It was actually built at *Kooryuak*, seven miles upriver, but Kittigazuit was better known, therefore its name was used to identify the location of the reindeer camp. According to Park Warden Victor Allen, *Kooryuak*, loosely translated, means "main channel" and *Kittigazuit* means "where the river fans out and is shallow".
2. Letter, Erling Porsild to O. S. Finnie, Jan. 14, 1931.
3. Letter, Bob Porsild to O. S. Finnie, Feb. 28, 1931.
4. Memo, Erling Porsild to O. S. Finnie, May 6, 1930.
5. Letter, Ralph Lomen to O. S. Finnie, Jan. 27, 1931.
6. The combination of wind and cold have been calculated and placed on charts in determining what today is called the "wind chill factor". For example, if the mercury is 40 below zero Fahrenheit, and the wind is blowing 40 miles per hour, the temperature equivalency is 115 below zero. At this level, exposed flesh will freeze within thirty seconds!
7. *The Great Trek*, Max Miller (New York: Doubleday, Doran, 1935), p. 152.
8. Letter of Andrew Bahr to Lomen Commercial Company, July 21, 1931.
9. The lemming's tiny bear-like tracks gave rise to his Eskimo name, *kilanmiutaurak*, "the little one who came down from the sky". According to native legend, the lemming was the size of a bear in the heavens, where he originally lived.

One day he slipped and fell from his lofty perch, becoming smaller as he plunged earthward. Finally, when he plopped into the snow on earth, he had diminished to his present size of from five to six inches in length.

10. In defence of the two Lapps, their gripes were not illegitimate. Poor food and raggedy foot gear, Bahr's sluggish pace, and his partiality to the Wood brothers grated on them to the point of distraction.
11. Letter, Andrew Bahr to the Lomen Commercial Company, July 21, 1931.
12. Wire from Jack Smith to Alfred Lomen, July 21, 1932.

CHAPTER 9 (p.161)

1. Memo, D. L. McKeand to J. Lorne Turner, Dec. 23, 1931.
2. Memo, H. E. Hume to H. H. Rowatt, Aug. 13, 1932.
3. Memo, J. Doyle to H. E. Hume, Aug. 13, 1932.

CHAPTER 10 (p.177)

1. Letter, Andrew Bahr to Alfred Lomen, July 25, 1932.
2. *The Great Trek*, p. 251.
3. See *Alone Across the Top of the World*, David Irwin as told to Jack O'Brien, (Chicago: John G. Winston, 1935). Irwin eventually reached the area of Franklin's debacle, but failed to solve the mystery. The veil was partially lifted with publication of *Frozen in Time*, Owen Beatty and John Geiger (Saskatoon: Western Producer Prairie Books, 1987).
4. *Alone Across the Top of the World*, p. 79–80.
5. *Alone Across the Top of the World.*

CHAPTER 11 (p.193)

1. Letter, Leonard Baldwin to H. E. Hume, Oct. 17, 1932.
2. Wire, Hume to Erling Porsild, Oct. 26, 1932.
3. Wire, Porsild to Hume, Nov. 5, 1932.
4. Memo, H. H. Rowatt to H. E. Hume, Nov. 5, 1932.
5. Calgary *Herald*, November 1, 1936.
6. Letter, Andrew Bahr to Ralph Lomen, March 7, 1933.
7. Wire, Bob Porsild to H. E. Hume, March 29, 1933.

CHAPTER 12 (p.209)

1. Drew University, *The Baldwin Legacy* (pamphlet).
2. *The Baldwin Legacy.*

3. Just about every major polar expedition experienced its share of internal trouble, even to the point of murder. This includes the alleged poisoning of Commander C.F. Hall by his physician in 1871. Over a century later, Hall's bones were examined and found to contain enough arsenic to have killed him. Another expedition that had its share of controversy was the Lady Franklin Bay group commanded by A.W. Greeley in 1882. One of the men, under starvation conditions, began to steal food from the larder. He was discovered and, since it was an army command, ordered confined to his sleeping bag pending court martial. He was found guilty and shot. Other notable feuds fostered in the Arctic included bitter rivalries between Cook and Peary, and Stefansson and Anderson.
4. Letter, Andrew Bahr to Ralph Lomen, May 21, 1933.
5. Letter, Dr. J. A. Urquhart to Erling Porsild, May 15, 1933.
6. Letter, Andrew Bahr to Ralph Lomen, May 21, 1933.
7. Polar bears are completely carnivorous, and unpredictable; thus with respect to man, they are one of the most dangerous animals in the world. The Lapps had increased their mobility by improvising ice skates before they set out. The blades were made from files, set on edge!
8. Wire, Erling Porsild to H. E. Hume, June 27, 1933. Also following extract.
9. Letter, H. E. Hume to Ralph Lomen, June 28, 1933.
10. Letter, Dan Crowley to Alfred Lomen, Sept.4, 1933. Following extract from the same letter.
11. Letter, Carl Lomen to Ralph Lomen, July 8, 1933.

CHAPTER 13 (p.227)

1. Bahr was not stingy with youngsters. Fred Inglangasuk recalled as a boy at Kay Point that Bahr gave him raisins which he liked for the sweet taste. Fred's aunt, Elizabeth, married herder Terrence Driggs.
2. *Alaska Reindeer Herdsmen*, Olson, p.28.
3. Dick Manixa (aka Maniksuk), an Inuit, had been one of the foremost harpoon men in the whaling fleet in the early 1900s. He was a powerful man, and so tall "you fell over when you looked at him". He later moved back to his cabin.
4. Letter, Andrew Bahr to Ralph Lomen, Jan. 19, 1934.
5. Letter, Andrew Bahr to Ralph Lomen, March 18, 1934.

6. Report, Canadian Legation, April 17, 1934.

CHAPTER 14 (p.248)

1. Letter, Dan Crowley to Ralph Lomen, July 1, 1934.
2. Letter, Andrew Bahr to Ralph Lomen, April 18, 1934.
3. Letter, Dan Crowley to Ralph Lomen, Jan. 12, 1935.
4. Letter, Mikkel Pulk to Mrs. Pulk, Jan. 18, 1935 (translation).
5. Crowley to Lomen, Jan. 12, 1935.
6. Letter, Ralph Lomen to Dan Crowley, April 18, 1935.
7. The final tally was: females (all ages) — 1498; bulls and yearlings — 289; steers — 261; male fawns — 322.

EPILOGUE (p.263)

1. Nasogaluak's financial advisor and business manager, Douglas Billingsley, also worked in the same capacity for the first private owner, Silas Kanagegana, who purchased the herd in 1974. They formed Canadian Reindeer Ltd., under which the reindeer business still operates. Billingsley advised the author in an interview that the herd is currently (1989) up for sale. The Inuvialuit Corporation of that region has displayed some interest in purchasing it with the idea of transplanting the deer to various settlements in the Canadian Arctic.

BIBLIOGRAPHY

GOVERNMENT DOCUMENTS

Canada

Public Archives of Canada, *National Resources Records.* File: 270-1-1, Vols. 1135 and 1136, Record Group 85.

Reindeer Grazing in Northwest Canada, Erling Porsild. King's Printer, Ottawa, 1929.

The Reindeer Industry and the Canadian Eskimo, Erling Porsild. Presented before the Geographic Society; published in *The Geographical Journal,* July 1936.

United States

Reindeer in Alaska, Seymour Hadwen and L. J. Palmer. Department of Agriculture, Bulletin No. 1069. Government Printing Office, September 22, 1922.

Percentage Marking of Reindeer, L. J. Palmer. Department of Agriculture, Government Printing Office, December 1926.

Progress of Reindeer Grazing Investigations in Alaska, L. J. Palmer. Bulletin No. 1423, Government Printing Office, October 1926.

The Introduction of Reindeer to Alaska, Bureau of Education, Annual Report, 1897–1898.

BOOKS

Alaska Geographic Society. *The Kotzebue Basin*. Anchorage: 1981.

Berton, Pierre. *Klondike*. Toronto: McClelland and Stewart, 1958.

Cunningham, John T. *University in the Forest*. Florham Park: Afton, 1972.

Evans, Allen Roy. *Reindeer Trek*. Toronto: McClelland and Stewart, 1935 (novel).

I, Nuligak. Markham: Simon and Schuster, 1966.

Irwin, David. *Alone Across the Top of the World*. Chicago: John C. Winston, 1935.

Lomen, Carl. *Fifty Years in Alaska*. New York: David McKay, 1954.

Miller, Max. *The Great Trek*. Garden City, New York: Doubleday, Doran, & Co., 1935.

Potter, Jean. *The Flying North*. Philadelphia: Curtis, 1947.

Proceedings of the Fourth International Reindeer/Caribou Symposium. Harstad, Norway: Nordic Council for Reindeer Research, 1986. Auspices of *Rangifer* Magazine.

Webster, D. H. and Zibell, W. *Inupiat Eskimo Dictionary*. Fairbanks: 1970.

PERIODICALS

American Game, June–July, 1930.

Canadian, November, 1929.

Canadian Boy, April 12, 1930.

Canadian Geographic, October–November, 1978.

Fur Farmer, November, 1927.

Journal of Geography, April, 1939.

Locomotive Engineers Journal, May, 1925.

National Geographic, March, 1972.

National Geographic, December, 1979.

National Geographic, February, 1983.

Saturday Night, February 8, 1930.

Scarlet & Gold, 16th Edition, 1935.

NEWSPAPERS

1926

"Plans Reindeer Week . . . ", *New York Times*, March 18.

"Study being Made . . . ", National Resources *Bulletin*, August.

"Will Experiment . . . ", Prince Albert *Herald*, November 6.

"Launches Plan to . . . ", Vancouver *Province*, November 7.

"Sees Arctic as . . . ", Vancouver *Province*, November 25.

1927

"The Reindeer Industry", Ottawa *Citizen*, June 14.

1928

"Airplanes Now Used . . . ", *New York Times*, January 13.

"Canada Imports Reindeer . . . ", *New York Times*, June 7.

"Alaska Reindeer for North Areas", Edmonton *Journal*, July 5.

"Waste Land and Wild Life", Ottawa *Journal*, October 12.

"New Paths are Blazed . . . ", Edmonton *Journal*, October 26.

"Pair Return . . . ", Montreal *Gazette*, October 22.

"Reindeer Ranching", Windsor Border Cities *Star*, October 22.

"Dr. Brown Inducted . . . ", *New York Times*, October 18.

"Survey Made of . . . ", Montreal *Gazette*, October 24.

"Government Plans to . . . ", Calgary *Albertan*, October 24.

"Return to Ottawa . . . ", Ottawa *Journal*, October 27.

"Brothers Complete . . . ", Toronto *Star*, October 27.

1929

"Reindeer Industry is Included", Vancouver *Province*, February 20.

"Prelude to Reindeer . . . ", *New York Times*, March 22.

"Deer Industry Possibilities . . . ", North Bay *Nugget*, March 26.

"Development of Northland", Victoria *Colonist*, April 5.

"Reindeer for the Northwest", Montreal *Gazette*, April 19.

"Canada Advances Reindeer Scheme", Quebec *Chronicle Telegraph*, May 31.

"Reindeer of Alaska . . . ", *New York Times*, June 9.

"Arrangements being Made," Moose Jaw *Times*, August 30.

"Great Reindeer Drive to Start", Ottawa *Citizen*, October 2.

"Drive Reindeer 1,500 Miles", Edmonton *Journal*, October 2.

"Planes to Aid Reindeer Drive", *New York Times*, October 3.

"Huge Reindeer Horde Ready", St. John *Telegraph*, October 9.
"A Minister of Venison", *The British Columbian*, New Westminster, October 6.
"Lomen Reindeer Drive", Nome *Nugget*, November.
"Reindeer Industry's Remarkable Growth", Strollers *Weekly*, November 2.
"Reindeer Meat", Winnipeg *Tribune*, November 4.
"Canada Plays Santa Claus", Victoria *Colonist*, December 20.

1930
"3,000 Reindeer . . . ", Victoria *Colonist*, March 2.
"3,400 Reindeer Start . . . ", Boston *Christian Science Monitor*, March 10.
"Fly North from Edmonton", Edmonton *Journal*, March 11.
"Interior Employee in Plane Crash", Ottawa *Journal*, March 18.

1931
"Reindeer Moving to Canada", *New York Times*, February 1.

1933
"The Most Spectacular Drive in Live Stock History", feature by Charles C. Cohan, Los Angeles *Sunday Times*, January 15.
"L. D. Baldwin, 64 . . . ", *New York Times*, January 26, 1933.
"Great Reindeer Trek and Epic . . . ", *New York Times*, May 4.
"Reindeer to the Rescue", feature by Lowell Thomas, Billings *Gazette*, no date.

1934
"Reindeer Herd", Ottawa *Journal*, March 5.
"Arrives in Ottawa . . . ", Ottawa *Journal*, April 4.
"Huge Herd Moved", Calgary *Herald*, September 27.
"Reindeer Trek Near End", *New York Times*, October 7.
"Reindeer Herd is . . . ", Ottawa *Citizen*, October 12.
"Herd of Reindeer . . . ", Calgary *Herald*, November 28.

1935
"Odyssey of Grit", Ottawa *Journal*, February 26.
"Big Herd of Reindeer . . . ", *New York Times*, February 26.
"Reindeer Herd Delivered", Edmonton *Journal*, March 15.
"New Reindeer Herd . . . ", Calgary *Herald*, March 17.
"Reindeer and Debate", feature by Will Rogers, Seattle *Times*, March 17.

"Reindeer Chief Tells . . . ", syndicated feature, North American Newspaper Alliance, March 31.
Assorted articles and features, Seattle *Times*, Seattle *Post Intelligencer*, March and April.
"Fate's Cruel Trick", Washington *Post*, June 16.
"Canada's Reindeer", Ottawa *Citizen*, November 21.

1936
"Reindeer for the Eskimo", editorial, Edmonton *Journal*, August 24.
"Epic Trek Proves . . . ", editorial, Ottawa *Citizen*, August 28.
"Predicts Reindeer Herd . . . ", Edmonton *Journal*, September 19.
"Hero of Big Reindeer Trek", Calgary *Herald*, October 31.

1938
"Reindeer 'Loan' to Aid . . . ", Toronto *Star*, September 14.
"Reindeer Rounded Up", Ottawa *Journal*, September 23.
"Another Reindeer Trek Planned", Ottawa *Journal*, November 15.

After
"Arthur J. Baldwin . . . ", *New York Times*, July 22, 1939.
"Canada's Reindeer . . . " Edmonton *Journal*, November 7, 1968.
"Herds Need Growing Room", Yellowknife *News of the North*, October 7, 1983.
"Laplanders Hope to . . . ", Whitehorse *Star*, October 29, 1986.
"Radioactive Leftovers . . . ", Toronto *Globe and Mail*, January 17, 1987.

ACKNOWLEDGEMENTS

The fundamental material for this work was obtained from the Public Archives of Canada. The PAC files contain over one thousand letters covering the period from 1922 to 1935. In addition, the archives furnished copies of thirty-eight original photos, copies of magazine stories, newspaper accounts, and government documents pertaining to the reindeer industry. In charge of this collection was Tom Nesmith, an indefatigable archivist, who at that time worked in the Natural Resources Record Section. His prompt and patient responses to my queries were greatly appreciated through the many years of our correspondence. Others who were of considerable help were Doug Whyte, Yves Marcoux, and Sheilah Powell.

I must thank Jean and Fred Francais, who initiated searches through the Westhampton Beach, New York Free Library, for tracking down information on the Baldwin brothers. Thanks also go to Priscilla Downs of that library, and Mark Rothenberg of the Suffolk County Cooperative Library

Service. Their assistance led me to Rachel M. Jones of Drew University, who forwarded additional valuable material.

Nancy Rickets, archivist at Sheldon Jackson College, uncovered rare historical information about Andrew Bahr and came up with some of the photos contained herein.

My gratitude is extended to Nels Nitchman of the United States Coast Guard Academy and to Paul Johnson, the Academy's archivist, for information concerning Lt. Bertolf's trip to purchase reindeer in Siberia.

Paul McCarthy, University of Alaska (Fairbanks) Archivist and Curator of Manuscripts helped through his detailed description of Lomen material available at the college. This led me to the Glenbow Museum, Calgary, Alberta, where Mrs. Lindsay Moir assisted in finding photos on hand there.

Yukon Archives is my traditional home base. The staff has always been accommodating on my many forays through their stacks of material. Northwest Territories Archives data was surprisingly sparse about the drive, but what they did have they quickly listed for me. I thank the Assistant Archivist, Richard Valpy, and Archival Assistant Janet Chatwood.

Credit should be given to my local library in Whitehorse, to Joy Wickett who has obtained microfilms for me from all over North America.

Interviewing Elly Porsild was like looking through a window into the past. Thanks to her I was able to see a way of life lost to the ages. And when I conversed with Andy Bangs (aka Bango) at his cabin behind Unalakleet, Alaska, he relived the heyday of the reindeer when over 100,000 of the deer were spread over the nearby hills. My interviews with Rhoda Allen and Elizabeth Driggs, widows of herders Edwin Allen and Terrence Driggs, were equally enlightening.

The Lomen brothers are gone now, but I corresponded with Al Lomen, the son of Alfred, who gave me a good rundown on his father's life as well as on his uncles. My interview with Bob Porsild was short. Possibly he was contemplating the idea of writing his own book about the drive, though he never did.

I should not neglect to mention my meeting with David Irwin, though I can hardly classify it as an interview. I was around ten or eleven years old when I went to the Grand Central Palace in New York City to see the annual sportsmen's show held there. I recall meeting Irwin, who was dressed in a light caribou or reindeer-skin parka. I obtained an autographed copy of his *Alone Across the Top of the World.* He had several sled dogs in hand. By the time I commenced research on the drive in the 1960s, I had long forgotten that Irwin had worked with Bahr for a short time on the drive.

Grateful for his assistance, but extremely sad that he died on almost the same day I completed this work, I found Richard Finnie to be a wealth of information about his father, O. S., and the north country in general.

Many other individuals rendered assistance through their insight, or knowledge of the drive and its participants. Vic Allen, who was raised in the vicinity of Herschel Island and is now a warden in the Yukon Territorial Park established there, cleared up some of the historical and geographical puzzles I encountered. Ann Kasook, program director for the Inuvialuit Communications Society, and the Society itself, are to be thanked for providing insight on the drive.

Willy Thomas, John Bottomley, Harlan Moen, Bradford Washburn, Thomas Arey, Jr., Knute Hansen, Dennis and Fred Inglangasuk, and Charlie Linklater were helpful.

Elizabeth Logue utilized her talents as an English major in proofing the manuscript, and her comments about the work were appreciated.

Always, it seems, that when giving credit someone is left out. Many, many persons have given help to me through quick critiques, a reference here, a suggestion there, a digression about a certain subject, a remembrance of some participant that sent me scurrying to a reference stack. I apologize to those I have not mentioned, though they know of my gratitude.

Lastly, the critical eyes of my wife, Andrée, sent me back to the re-write table again and again. Her pertinent comments were always welcomed.

I would be remiss if I did not mention the Eagle Plains Hotel, situated on a ridge only twenty miles from the Arctic Circle on the Dempster Highway.

I thank George McNevin and his family, owners and operators of the hotel, for their hospitality and for honouring me as their official "Writer in Residence."

Finally, Editor Sheldon Fischer's patience and tenacity in working with the author to make the manuscript readable was invaluable. To all of these, my thanks.

INDEX